Quest for Identity in Contemporary Indian English Drama

Quest for Identity in Contemporary Indian English Drama

A.J. Sebastian sdb

ADHYAYAN

ADHYAYAN PUBLISHERS & DISTRIBUTORS

NEW DELHI (INDIA)

Published by

ADHYAYAN PUBLISHERS & DISTRIBUTORS

4378/4B, 105, J.M.D. House, Murari Lal Street
Ansari Road Darya Ganj, New Delhi - 110002
Ph.: 011-23263018, 011-23277156, Fax: 011-23280028
Email: adhyayanpublishers@yahoo.com

Quest for Identity in Contemporary Indian English Drama

Edition 2011
ISBN 978-81-8435-254-2

Printed in India

Published by Harish Chandra Yadav for Adhyayan Publishers & Distributors, Laser Typeseting at A.V. Rao and Printed at Tarun Offset Printers, Delhi

Acknowledgements

I owe a great deal of gratitude to several people who have helped me in writing this book. I thank God for his bounty and blessing while pursuing my endeavours. I register my gratitude to my brother Rev. Antony Aelavanthara who has been the motivating force behind this project.

I remember with gratitude my Superiors, family, friends and well-wishers who have helped me in manifold ways. I am grateful to Dr. Nigamananda Das who carefully checked the manuscripts and Mr. H.C. Yadav, M/s Adhyayan Publishers & Distributors, New Delhi for publishing the book with keen interest.

Kohima
24 November 2010

A.J. Sebastian sdb

INTRODUCTION

I

Identity in general describes a person's conception and expression of his/her individuality or group affiliations including national_ and cultural identity. The term has its nuances in psychology and sociology. A person's *psychological identity* relates to his/her self-image, self-esteem, and individuality. Gender identity is an important part of one's psychology as it dictates to a great extent how one views himself/herself both as a person and in relation to other people, ideas and nature. In cognitive psychology, the term "identity" refers to the capacity for self-reflection and the awareness of self (Leary 3). For psychologists "identity" describes *personal_identity* or the idiosyncratic things that make a person unique. Sociologists on the other hand stress *social identity* of a person as a member of a group that defines him/her as an individual.

It was Erik Erikson who explored to a great extent the psychological concept of identity. He makes a distinction between the *ego identity* or "the self"; *personal identity* (that separates one person from the other wit his/her personal idiosyncrasies); and the *social identity* or the *cultural identity* by which a person plays social roles. Erikson traces the identity formation across a person's lifespan. According to him the development of a strong ego identity, along with the proper integration into a stable society and culture, leads to a stronger sense of identity in general. Accordingly, a deficiency in either of these factors may increase the chance of an identity crisis or confusion (Cote 22).

Canadian developmental psychologist, James Marcia has furthered the "Neo-Eriksonian" *identity status* paradigm focussing upon the twin concepts of *exploration* and *commitment.* The central idea is that any individual's sense of identity is determined largely by the choices and commitments made regarding certain personal and social traits. It follows that the core of the research in this paradigm investigates the degrees to which a person has made certain explorations, and the degree to which he or she displays a commitment to those explorations.

A person may display either relative weakness or relative strength in terms of both exploration and commitments. When assigned categories, four possible permutations result: identity diffusion, identity foreclosure, identity moratorium, and identity achievement. Diffusion is when a person lacks both exploration in life and interest in committing even to those unchosen roles that he or she occupies.

The core idea is that one's sense of identity is determined largely by the choices and commitments made regarding certain personal and social traits. The work done in this paradigm considers how much one has made certain choices, and how much he or she displays a commitment to those choices. Identity involves the adoption of i) a sexual orientation, ii) a set of values and ideals and iii) a vocational direction. A well-developed identity gives on a sense of one's strengths, weaknesses, and individual uniqueness. A person with a less well-developed identity is not able to define his or her personal strengths and weaknesses, and does not have a well articulated sense of self. (Marcia 551-558).

There are also some social psychology theories that attempt to deal with the issue of identity at both the levels of individual cognition and of collective behaviour. In the Social Identity Theory, a person has not one, "personal self", but rather several selves that correspond to widening circles of group membership. Different social contexts may trigger an individual to think, feel and act on basis of his personal, family or national "level of self" (Turner et al, 1987). Apart from the "level of self", an individual has multiple "social identities". Social identity is the individual's self-concept derived from perceived membership of social groups (Hogg & Vaughan)

Anthropologists have most frequently employed the term 'identity' to refer to this idea of selfhood in a loosely Eriksonian way, based on the uniqueness of individuals in the wake of contemporary social movements.

The theme of identity is often expressed in literature. Though Contemporary Indian English has been on the decine in the recent past due to the onslaught of Television and film, dramatists have dared to write and perform their plays mingled with regional traditions and societal concerns.

II

The essays in this anthology on select plays of contemporary dramatists, are an attempt to read their protagonists' quest for identity in the midst of multiple interactions. They have sought different modes of expression – from conventional to non conventional, absurd to expressionistic – studded with irony, subtle humour and evoking pathos, sympathy and laughter. Some of the papers that have appeared earlier in journals and anthologies have been updated and enlarged.

Mahesh Dattani's *Final Solutions* probes into unchecked communalism gnawing into secular fabric of India, disturbing its peace and harmony. In *Tara* the playwright draws attention to real scenario of gender discrimination in our society. And *Where There is a Will* traces issues of patriarchal hegemony.

In *The Cyclewallah* Vijay Tendulkar examines the existential human predicament and absurdities of life, while In *Silence! The Court is in Session* he investigates how a corrupt legal system victimises a young woman.

Asif Currimbhoy has been very prolific in exploring human predicament through his social, moral religious and political concerns in his plays. In *Inquilab (Revolution)* the dramatist depicts the Naxalite struggle in Bengal, probing into the reign of terror unleashed. **In *The Dissident M.L.A.* Currimbhoy surveys the political instability let loose in Gujarat.**

Sriranga's analysis of human psychology and social ethos is examined in *Shadows in the Dark, Agnisakshi, Yama Vanquished* and *Ramarajya.*

In his *Wedding Album,* Girish Karnard explores appearance and reality, giving insights into contemporary middle-class Indian society in the wake of technological advancement.

Badal Sircar's *Life of Bangla* explores how human will and determination alone can make one stand on his own feet instead of living in a make-believe world of magic. The dramatist reaches out to his audience with a moral lesson in establishing one's own identity as a worthwhile human being, shedding built in inferiority complex under whatever oppressive circumstances.

Class Antagonism is the pivot of Manoj Mitra's *Honey from a Broken Hive* where the dramatist responds to politically motivated violence and killing of landlords.

In *Garbo* Mahesh Elkunchwar probes into the meaningless lives young people live, in our contemporary society, devoid of social and ethical values.

The dramatists have been unique in their powerful portrayal of human passions, virtues and vices, depicting at the same time characters from the various strata of society.

Works Cited:

Cote, James E. & Levine, Charles. *Identity Formation, Agency, and Culture*. New Jersey: Lawrence Erlbaum Associates, 2002.

Hogg, M.A. & Vaughan, G.M. *Social Psychology (3rd ed.)* London: Prentice Hall, 2002.

Leary, M. R.& Tangney, J. P. *Handbook of Self and Identity*. New York: Guilford Press, 2003.

Marcia, J. E.. "Development and validation of ego identity status." *Journal of Personality and Social Psychology*. 3, 1966, 551-558.

Contents

1

Religious Bigotry in Mahesh Dattani's *Final Solutions*

India has been plagued by unchecked communalism since its independence, gnawing into the very fabric of secularism, peace and harmony that existed from time immemorial. We are getting torn apart by communal hatred and carnage, perpetrated in the name of religious affiliations. The ugly face of this diabolic trend emerges from within human hearts devoid of love of God and man. Dattani has powerfully brought out the scenario of religious bigotry in *Final Solutions* portraying construction of Communalism in India.

Sudhir Kakar's psychoanalyst's exploration of religious conflict between Hindus and Muslims through a case study of the violence that erupted in Hyderabad in 1990s, may aptly be applied to the play. Dattani has based his story on the events after partition. As has been pointed out, "...historical enmity is transmitted from one generation to the next as the child ignoring the surface interpretations and rationalizations, hears the note of helpless fury and impotence in the accounts of beloved adults and fantasizes scenarios of revenge against those who have humiliated family and kin" (Kakar 31). Such is the case in hand when Hardika recounts from the past her bitterness in the play. The psychology of rioting may be examined briefly to assess the play:

> ...a riot has a period of *immediate tension* and *precipitating incident* which have received much glamorous search for "ultimate" causes. The build up of immediate tension occurs when religious identities come to the fore front because of a perceived threat to this particular social identity...the threat... makes

members of the community demonstratively act through words and actions as Hindus, or as Muslims" (Kakar 41).

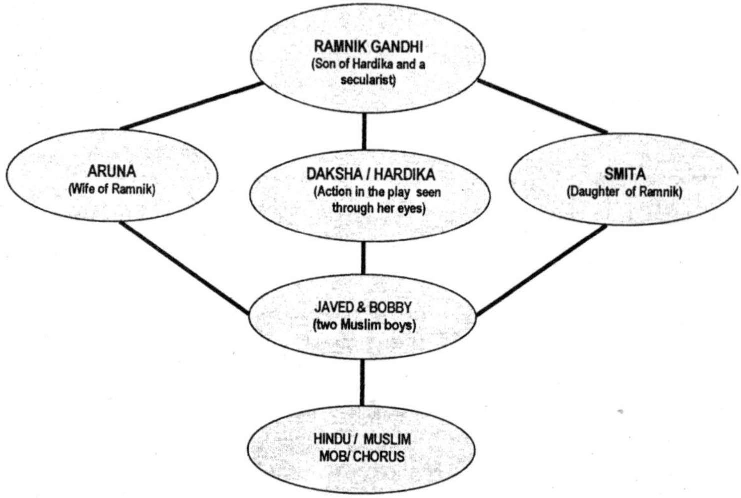

Final Solutions is a memory play. Dattani employs Chorus/Mob consisting of five men and ten masks on sticks - five Hindu masks and five Muslim masks. As individuals they are Chorus 1,2, etc. The period of the play is the late 1940s when the fifteen year old Daksha reads from her diary. She jots down how her dreams have been shattered. She had been told not to sing after her marriage to Hari. It was the time when India got her independence. She reads from her diary reminiscing the terrible times of India's independence. The trauma of partition looms large as she recounts her thoughts. Through time shift, the playwright presents the mindset of three generations of a middle-class Gujarati business family. Daksha growing up to be the grandmother Hardika, remembers vividly her father's murder during partition riots. She recollects:

> But that night in Hussainabad in our ancestral house... The windows broke, one by one. My mother and myself, we hid in the pooja room... I clung to my mother. My mother clung to the family idol of Lord Krishna... I could see the fire they were carrying... I looked at my mother praying, with her eyes tightly shut, clutching the feet of the idol, praying not for us but for the safety of my father, wherever he may be.... I had the most

> horrible thought…Then I knew it was Krishna slapping me in the face, punishing me for being a non-believer. A stone hit our gramophone table, breaking it. Krishna chose to destroy what I loved most (*FS* 167).

Her son Ramnik Gandhi, aware of the cruelty perpetrated by his forebears, wants to live in the true spirit of secularism.

The scene shifts to forty years later when Hardika opens her diary and feels that "things have not changed that much" (167). Dattani brings in Mob/Chorus wearing Hindu masks discussing how the procession of the God in the chariot was disrupted by the Muslims, pelting stone at the God and slitting the poojari's stomach. The infuriated mob scattered with sticks cries blood.

> CHORUS 4: Send them back
> CHORUS 2: Drive..them…out.
> CHORUS 5: Drive them out?
> CHORUS 3: Kill the sons of swine! (169).

The scene shifts to the living room of the Gandhis where they have received news over TV of the riots. Smita is all excited while dialling to inform her friend Tasnee's parents about the bombing of the Muslim girls' hostel. Ramnik takes over the phone, though unknown to Tasnee's father Noor Ahmed, to inform him of the blast. Making the conversation sound more humorous, he introduces himself as Gandhi, having no relation, of course, to the father of the nation. However, he attempts to reach out like a true Gandhian to members of the Muslim community. On the other hand, the Muslim masked Mob/ Chorus takes up the chorus of retaliation:

> CHORUS 1:Their chariot fell in our street!
> CHORUS 2:Their God now prostrates before us!…
> CHORUS 3:They say we razed their temples yesterday.
> CHORUS 2:That we broke their chariot today.
> CHORUS 1:That we'll bomb their streets tomorrow.
> CHORUS ALL:Why would we? Why? Why? Why would we? (171).

Resorting to time switch, Dattani focuses on Hardika recollecting her fears: "This time it wasn't the people with the sticks and stones. It was those two boys running away who frightened me. Those two who were begging for their lives. Tomorrow they will hate us for it…All those memories came back when I saw the pride in their eyes!... They don't want equality. They want to be superior" (172). She reminisces her bitter past and continues to cherish an unforgiving spirit filled with suspicion and fear.

In the meantime, the dramatist draws our attention to the religious fervour of Aruna who does her pooja meticulously along with her daughter Smita to get protection from Krishna. She tells her to be always pure in thought and deeds.

The drama moves on to the scene of the two Muslim boys, Bobby and Javed, trying to escape from the Hindu mob. When the mob/chorus interrogates them, their Muslim identity is revealed. They have no other choice but to make their escape for survival. The Mob/Chorus wearing Hindu masks chase them shouting "Drive them out! Kill the sons of swine!" (178). The duo come to the door of the Gandhi household appealing for mercy and shelter. In his goodness Ramnik opens the door with due hesitation. At the background Daksha and Hardika are shown raising their objection to his ushering in the boys whose community killed Ramnik's own grandfather. As the Gandhis are engaged in conversation with the two boys, the mob wearing Muslim masks express their anxiety as they are hunted down, beaten and thrown out. They express their strength though they are few in number.

As Bobby and Javed plead for protection and shelter from Ramnik, the Hindu Mob/Chorus outside demands that the intruders be let out.

> CHORUS ALL: Thwart them. So we may live in peace.
> RAMNIK: We?
> CHORUS ALL: We who are right.
> RAMNIK: And they?
> CHORUS ALL: They who are wrong. Since we are right. And they oppose us.
> ...
> RAMNIK: I will not open the door! Go away!
> CHORUS ALL: We shall break in then!
> RAMNIK: I stand in front of the door. If you break the door, you will kill me.
> CHORUS ALL: What? You protect them? Then you are a traitor! Traitor! (181).

When the argument heats up, Aruna insists that her husband surrender the boys. However, Ramnik spares them as the duo keep pleading for safety. As the Mob/Chorus leave, Ramnik begins his interrogation. He learns that they are college students. Smita recognizes them as her college pals.

Act II continues with the interrogation of the boys where Smita reveals how she knew them both. Javed is her friend Tasneem's brother and Bobby has been Tasneem's fiance. The argument leads to exchanges between the two parties, leading Ramnik to tell them not to leave his home in the night. Javed realizes his mistake in arguing and apologises for his ungrateful and angry expressions.

Meanwhile when a stone is hurled at his house, Ramnik blames it on Javed's people and goes on to refer to violence of the past when Hardika lost her father in Hussinabad soon after partition. The spotlight falls on Hardika who is angry with Ramnik being blinded by his ideals, offering shelter to the Muslim boys even offering jobs.

Ramnik tells the boys not to take seriously the comments of the grandmother since old people are too rigid about things, unlike the young people like them. Bringing two glasses of milk to them, Ramnik insists Javed takes his offer of a job expressing his principle: "…if you want peace…that is, if you treat peace as a commodity and you look for it – you will find it hidden in the armpits of the majority" (191). Javed acknowledges Ramnik's humanitarian gesture in the midst of violence and social tension. "…You can offer milk to us. You can have an angry mob outside your house. You can play the civilized host. Because you know you have peace hidden inside your armpit" (192).

To Javed's query about trouble fermenting in that big mohalla, Ramnik recounts how there was only a single Muslim family years back. It was an yearly practice to conduct rath yatra from Vishnu Mandir before midnight. In the course of the procession someone threw stones at the idol. The axle of the chariot gave way and broke the idol. It was also rumoured that the poojari was killed.

In his generosity, Ramnik offers Javed a job in his saree shop. Smita objects to the proposal and reveals how she came to know from Tasneem that Javed was driven out of his home by his father since he used to be hired to create riots. Feeling betrayed by the disclosure, Javed, keeps pounding his forehead with his fist.

Act III opens with the spotlight on Javed and Bobby, sitting on the floor, with troubled countenance. The Muslim Chorus is seated in prayerful posture on the highest level of the ramp. As the Chorus finishes praying, it expresses its fears and premonitions:

> CHORUS 1: Should we be swallowed up? Till they cannot recognize us? Should we melt into anonymity so they cannot hound us? Lose ourselves in a shapeless mass? Should we?... A drop of oil cannot merge with an ocean of milk. One reality cannot accept another reality (196).

The focus shifts to Daksha reading from her diary jottings. She was told by her husband Hari that violence had stopped and all the bad people had left for Pakistan. Hari wanted to give up studies and join his father in his cloth mill. She also recalls how her friend Zarine's family got into financial trouble.

The spotlight turns on to Ramnik, Javed and Bobby. When Ramnik questions Javed on his riot links, in anger he retorts, "Thousands! I got thousands, lakhs for doing it…That's what you want to hear!...I believe in myself… It's people like you who drive me to a corner and I have to turn to myself and my faith. I have a lot to thank you for! At least now I am not ignorant of my history and faith" (197-8).

Ramnik keeps his composure and invites him still to take the job in his shop, provided he changes his ways. The argument between the two continues as Javed accuses Ramnik of provoking him to do anti-social activities. Enraged, Ramnik points out how Javed grooms violence in himself: "How dare you blame your violence on other people? It is in you! You have violence in your mind. Your life is based on violence. Your faith is based…" (198). He stops abruptly, realizing his mistake and apologises. But as Javed further attacks him for his attitude, Ramnik slaps him calling him a criminal who cannot justify being a riot-rouser. Javed keeps arguing, further attacking him on his pretended liberal outlook, "You don't hate me for what I do or who I am. You hate me because I showed you that you are not as liberal as you think you are" (199). As Javed walks away to get fresh air, Bobby explains to Ramnik that Javed was not hired, but he did everything voluntarily. Ramnik calls his activities unforgivable. Yet he is willing to give Javed a chance to change his life, offering a job at the shop. Bobby finds it paradoxical on the part of Ramnik to offer a job to a fellow who has done such hateful things.

Ramnik defends himself, establishing his liberal mindedness: "I have to give him all the chances that I can possibly give. Isn't that what any liberal-minded person should do?" (199).

Bobby then reveals the real facts behind Javed's strange behaviour. It happened that once while playing cricket with friends, when the postman passed by, he happened to drop a letter. Noticing it, he requested Javed to hand it over to the addressee next door. Bobby and friends watched the neighbour telling Javed to leave the letter on the wall. Then the boys watched the man coming out with a cloth in hand, wiping the letter before picking it up. He also wiped the wall. The postman perceiving it merely grinned and told the boys the man was cracked. Then the boys could hear the continuous ringing of a prayer bell.

The following morning, the neighbour came out cursing everyone saying that someone had dropped pieces of meat and bones into his compound. Bobby never spoke to Javed about it, but remembered the incident whenever the ringing of the bell occurred while playing cricket. From then on, Javed was no more considered a hero among his peers. He knows that Javed expressed his disgust for the Hindu concept of contamination through retaliation.

Bobby eventually began to be angry with Javed whenever he heard the ringing of the bell. He began to pretend that he was not part of his community by changing his name to Bobby from Baboon. By and by, Ramnik realises his own mistaken viewpoint and finds no difference between him and the boys.

The focus shifts to Daksha who dances in her room with delight since she could visit her Muslim friend Zarine. She learnt that her father had suspected that his shop was burnt down by someone. He had been discussing something with his community men when Daksha visited their home one day. They abruptly changed the topic of their discussion seeing her and showing some indifference. It was only when Zarine's mother came and welcomed with a smile, she felt at ease. Daksha spent time with Zarine listening to Noor Jahan's songs on the gramophone which her mother-in-law never permitted her at home.

The spotlight falls on the trio continuing their argument, as Javed decided to leave the security of Ramnik's home in the night itself. Ramnik threatens Javed that he would hand him over to police calling him a criminal. Javed retorts sarcastically:

> You want to throw me to the mob? I am a part of it. You have been protecting me from the people like me. I'm not different from them!... I do what they are doing – only on a different street! I was there on that street when the rath came and I did precisely that! I shouted! I had permission to do exactly what I had been asked not to do all my life! ... They always talked about motherland and fighting to save our faith and how we should get four of theirs for every one of ours... it is obvious that a minority would never start a riot, we are too afraid, that it had to be politically motivated. Try telling it to a thousand devotees swayed by their own religious fervour, united by their fantasies of persecution, constantly reassuring themselves that this is their land by taking out processions (204-5).

It is in these circumstances of being hunted by enemies that Javed joined the riot makers who came by bus to pelt stones at the rath yatra. Though Bobby tried to dissuade Javed from his criminality, he went ahead in the midst of the chaotic situation. He had the knife in hand lifted up to plunge into the poojari who begged for mercy. But enveloped in fear, he had no courage to move his hands in confusion. Dropping the knife, trying to make a safe exit, he observed someone pick up the knife and pierce the poojari. Listening to their pathetic story, Ramnik felt glad they managed to escape from the riot.

The spotlight falls on the Muslim Chorus that expresses its angst and fears:

> CHORUS 1: What must we do? To become more acceptable? Must we lose our identity? Is that what they want? Must we tolerate more? Does our future lie in their hands? Is there anyone more unsure more insecure than us? Or what a curse it is to be less in number! (208).

The cross-fade to the living room, bringing to picture Smita and Aruna, in conversation with Javed. They apologise to each other for the miscommunications. Aruna expresses they have no ill feelings towards them and refers to their peculiar ways and customs. She acknowledges the unity of all religions with different pathways to God. Hearing this Ramnik laughs at her traditional attitudes he has never succeeded to change. She holds on to her conviction of bathing her God with uncontaminated water. Hence she didn't want Javed to fetch water from the tap outside. Observing this attitude of Aruna, Smita feels suffocated in her ideals. Aruna still keeps to her convictions saying, "We must know no other path. And I will not have it all perish to accommodate someone else's faith. I have enough faith and pride to see that it doesn't happen. I shall uphold what I believe is the truth" (210).

Smita on the other hand retorts questioning her mother's stifling faith. She draws her mother's attention to go beyond pettiness: " Do two young boys make you so insecure?... This is the time for strength! I am so glad these two dropped in. We would never have spoken about what makes us so different from each other. We would have gone on living our lives with our petty similarities" (211). This section focuses on the ritualistic practices of Aruna being questioned by the new generation that is more open to accommodation and friendship, going beyond mere rituals.

The spotlight passes on to Hindu Chorus which gives its response to the attitudes represented in the ensuing discussion in Ramnik household. The Chorus has its fears and predicaments: "Our future is threatened. There is so much that is fading away. We cannot be complacent about our glorious past seeing us safely through" (212). The Chorus is very anxious about the half hearted pseudo-secularists who do not know the greatness of the motherland.

Ramnik on his part appreciates Javed for his individuality trying to protect his interests with his angry, impulsive and rebellious attitudes. However, he advises him not to be stupid in his actions.

The conversation shifts to Javed, Smita and Bobby on the ramp. Javed asks Smita if she continues to love Bobby, since his sister Tasneem was in love with him too. Smita tells Bobby that she cannot continue her relationship with him for personal reasons, and not because of communal differences that she feared would invite problems. She also tells him that if they wanted they could have continued the relationship between them despite all odds. But since Bobby had made the choice otherwise, she willingly relented.

As the conversation winds up, Javed asks Smita if she had filled water to bathe the God. She, instead, wanted him to fill the water to prove that nothing would happen by his touch, bringing curse on the family. This is a breaking point in establishing fresh relationships among the new generation.

The sequence shifts to Daksha reading from her diary jotting about her husband Hari wanting to help Zarine's father by purchasing his burnt up little shop. But the man demanded too much for it which she condemns as false pride. It is in this background the spotlight shifts to Hardika questioning the two boys why they were still there and had not left the place. She asks them if they would leave for Pakistan so that they could live the way they liked without having to blame others for their failures. She recounts what her family did many years ago by leaving Hussainabad when her father was killed. The boys do not want to listen to those stories. Javed quietly says, "You blame us for what happened fifty years ago. Today, if something happens to my sister, can I blame you?" (222). Hardika doesn't show any concern but merely says, "What happened to your sister doesn't concern me! … She deserves it! Your sister deserves it! Zarine deserves… What did you say your sister's name was?" (222). The conversations shifts back to Daksha discussing with her husband Hari on her friendship with Zarine, promising that she would never visit her again.

The focus further shifts to Ramnik and Hardika. Ramnik tells his mother not to blame the boys, but she insists that she cannot forget the bitter past. After an ominous silence Bobby and Javed are seen visibly defeated. Meanwhile Aruna enters after her ritual bath to the pooja room and kneels. She rings the bell dispelling the silence. Bobby and Javed turn away to the door. Javed stops to stare to the direction of the bell that is being rung to waken the God. Bobby removes his footwear and advances towards the pooja room telling Javed, "There is one final deed to be done… God knows, my intentions are pure… It has to be done to prove to them… That we also believe" (223-4). Aruna tells him to stop, but he suddenly picks up the tiny image of Krishna which sits in his palm. Aruna's cry telling him to put it back is drowned by the Mob/Chorus. He shows the image to everyone and proclaims:

> See! I am touching God!... Your God! My flesh is holding Him! Look, Javed! And He does not mind!... He does not burn me to ashes! Her does not cry out from the heavens saying He has been contaminated!... Look how He rests in my hands! He knows I cannot harm Him. He knows His strength! I don't believe in

> Him but He believes in me. He smiles! He smiles at our trivial pride and our trivial shame... He doesn't cringe from my touch (224).

Though the Mob/Chorus keeps pounding and shouting not to hurt its pride by his sacrilege, Aruna keeps swearing that there is nothing that is sacred left in the world. Holding the image of Krishna, Bobby responds:

> You can bathe Him day and night, you can splash holy water on Him but you cannot remove my touch from His form. You cannot remove my smell with sandal paste... because it belongs to a human being who believes, and tolerates, and respects what other human beings believe... The tragedy is that there is too much that is sacred. But if we understand and believe in one another, nothing can be destroyed (224-5).

Bobby is willing to forget and tolerate provided Hardika is willing to do the same. But the old woman could never be willing to forget. She believes in living in isolation and move in silence unwilling to speak. As she walks to the living room, Ramnik tells her that he can't enter his shop thinking about the incident. He feels there is no escape from the contradiction of his life. He further reveals the mystery surrounding his shop: "It's the same burnt-up shop we bought from them, at half its value. And we burnt it. Your husband. My father. And his father. They had it burnt in the name of communal hatred" (226).

Now, conscience pricked, he can't step into the same shop. He thought he would settle matters with the boys who came, telling them that they are not the only ones who destroyed. He tells his mother that those people didn't hate her holding on to any false pride or arrogance.

The play ends with Hardika expressing her regret for not being told the truth of the fact and enquires if the boys would ever return. Ramnik merely says, "If you call them they will come. But then again – if it's too late – they may not" (226).

Dattani draws attention to inherent evil being perpetrated in the name of religious bickering and historical wounds inflicted. Can't it stop somewhere? Can't the new generation make a leap of faith in each other burying the hatchet in a forgive-forget basis. Hardika can't forget the past and forgive, but Bobby calls for understanding and deposit faith in one another to bridge the divide between communities.

"History" is made as an active character in the play making the action progress through the perception of Daksha/Hardika, mingling both the past and the present (Multani 110). Blaming it on history isonly a sign of lacking mature attitudinal change. It is same as holding fast to the age old adage, "The fathers have eaten a sour grape and the children's teeth are set on edge" (Jeremiah 31.19).

Can there be a final solution? The characters in the play are very deftly set apace from each other. The closer they come the better the interaction and sharing of sensibilities and emotions. The Mob/ Chorus remains at the periphery on the ramp who are only intruders, causing riots and tension, acting on impulses and mob frenzy. But the characters in the Gandhi household as they debate and argue, enter into better understanding. Javed and Bobby as they come to closer interaction, breaking off from the mob, are able to build a relationship with the Gandhi household. When Bobby forcefully enters into the inner space of the pooja room, he shatters the ritualistic outlook of religion.

The stage setting with multiple layers and distinctive zones in the backdrop of a riot-torn city, Dattani very powerfully projects how the ghosts of the past continue to haunt us through various characters, applying time-shift device. The drama searches for solutions to individual/ familial/ communal/ national issues ending with the younger generation carrying much less of the historical burden of their predecessors (Chaudhuri 39-40).

There is need to break the barriers created as "us" and "they" into "we" Indians, respecting one another as fellow country men, lest we perish with an eye for an eye attitude leading to a blind world.

Finally Dattani breaks into the core of Hardika who keeps the guarded historical grudge. She opens up finally, when truth is revealed. Ramnik's lack of proper communication of history is demonic as it kept up unquenched rancour and hatred. Truth, if revealed at the appropriate time can build relationship among warring parties. This is probed into in the play as it is an example of transferred resentments (Barbuddhe 103).

Though the play ends with no final solution, it is a critique of communal tension and rioting in India, calling for introspection on the part of every right thinking citizen, be it Hindu or Muslim, to build bridges of friendship and harmony. Mirroring our social tension, it draws out attention to the aftermath of our partition history, which continues unabated in subtle destruction of our social harmony. In the final analysis, rancour and hatred blooming in the human heart, unless nipped in the bud, will continue to spread like gangrene.

Final Solutions proves that "The Demons of communal hatred are not out on the street… they are lurking inside ourselves" (*FS* 161) Being a memory play, social introspection should lead to wiping the memories of the past with courage and determination to start anew to end all strife. Final solution is to break out of the demons lodged within human heart. If man has to live in peace, heart needs purification of hatred and evil sowing seeds of communal disharmony.

Works Cited

Barbuddhe, Satish. "Mahesh Dattani's *Final Solutions*: A Play about Transferred Resentments."

The Plays of Mahesh Dattani. Ed. R.K. Dhawan & Tanu Pant. New Delhi: Prestige Books,005, 98-103.

Bible, The Holy. Revise Standard Version. London: The Catholic Trust Society, 1966.

Chaudhuri, Asha Kuthari. *Mahesh Dattani.* New Delhi: Foundation Books, 2005.

Dattani, Mahesh."Final Solutions." *Collected Plays.* New Delhi: Penguin Books, 2000, 159-226. (Abbreviated *FS*)

Kakar, Sudhir. *The Colours of Violence*: *Cultural identities, religion and conflict*. Chicago: The University of Chicago Press, 1996.

Multani, Angelie. " "Final Solutions?" *Mahesh Dattani's Plays: Critical Perspectives.* Ed. Angelie Multani. New Delhi: Pencraft International, 2007, 109-21.

2

Guilt and Atonement in Mahesh Dattani's *Tara*

1. Introduction

When Mahesh Dattani (1958 -) was awarded Sahitya Akademi in 1998, the citation acknowledged his contribution to Indian drama as he "probes tangled attitudes in contemporary India towards communal differences, consumerism and gender...." He has been concerned with social issues purging any society with its unfortunate victims. *Tara* explores the reality of gender discrimination in a society that ill-treats its girl children. The situation is made graver when the child in question is physically challenged and denied opportunities. Her physical and emotional trauma leads her to waste away her life and die.

He has drawn attention to 'real scenarios that are tough to turn away from' and leads his readers/audience to 'shy away from myth and make-believe to tackle reality head-on, no matter what the impact of collision' (De 7 August). The trauma that the characters undergo brings effective catharsis in the audience. He has also been very effective with his stage techniques as he asserted: "Regarding my plays I try not to be didactic and allow the story/dramatic conflict to remain in the forefront" (Sebastian 28 November).

Erin Mee has rightly pointed out that *Tara* is "a play about the gendered self, about coming to terms with the feminine side of oneself in a world that always favours what is 'male'; but many in India see it as a play about the girl child" (*CP* 320). *Tara* is a powerful critique of socio-cultural evils associated with gender discrimination in Indian society. It climaxes tragically as it portrays the characters in angst as they grapple with guilt and atonement.

Dattani presents the play in memory with reminiscent scenes seen through light effects and music. The dramatist uses expressionistic technique with psychological presentation of characters (Sebastian 2002: 143). The play begins with Dan (Chandan) speaking to the audience: "Yes. I have my memories. Locking myself in a bedsitter in a seedy suburb of London, thousands of miles from home hasn't put enough distance between us... Twinkle Tara. A drama in two acts by Chandan Patel" (*CP* 324).

The opening statement of Dan is spoken from the inside of his head. His realistic life is one of struggle with his own memories of the past. He tries to forget the pain by consuming liquor. He wants to get back to his memories and "spit out the result to the world, in anger" (379). It is with this aim in mind he begins to write the story sitting in his London apartment trying to set his 'anguish into drama.'

We find Dan miming with masks on his face. He finds it very difficult to shed the last mask since he took two years to acquire it. Mask in the play is indicative of his hidden self and psychological break-down. He envelops his anguish by masking (Rani 10 December) and says: "And what remains is what I intend making capital of my freakishness. I am a freak.... Allow the memories to flood in. To tell you the truth, I had even forgotten I had a twin sister....Or maybe I didn't forget her. She was lying deep inside, out of reach" (*CP* 324).

He was broken by the tragic death of Tara and felt himself a freak in his guilt and helplessness. Now as he tries to write the play, memories of the past keep flooding his mind. Dan's mental confusion is similar to Tom in Tennessee Williams' *The Glass Menagerie*, the influence of which Dattani acknowledged: "Yes!, Tennessee Williams was a major influence in my formative years. *Tara* is probably the most obvious example of it" (Sebastian 28 November).

The dramatist employs Expressionism, depicting emotional experience in its most compelling form, aiming to create a totally unified stage picture that would increase the emotional impact on the audience. The attention of the audience is drawn to the inner working of the character's mind and the subconscious with subjective psychological analysis (Sebastian 88) "expressing immediate perception and building on more complex psychic structures" (Matejcek 175).

2. Application of the theory of love

In my assessment I apply Sternberg's theory of love with its variations (Answer.com). Sternberg examines love from three components: intimacy, passion, and decision/commitment. These may operate in combination or separately from one another. Accordingly, love can be classified into seven distinct kinds as shown in the chart below. The different kind of loves lets individuals to understand and communicate the types of emotional behaviours they express. Consummate love is the ideal and complete love, combining intimacy, passion and commitment (Sternberg).

The characters in their interpersonal relationship can be analysed applying the triangular theory of love propounded by psychologist Robert Sternberg. The theory of love is characterised by three different components.

Patel's love for his wife begins in *empty love* as it is characterized by commitment without much intimacy. But towards the end of the play when she becomes almost a neurotic, he is more compassionate in developing a *companionate* form of love for his wife. Mutual love between Tara and Chandan may be termed *consummate love* representing an ideal relationship.

Dr. Thakkar is set in the *nonlove* category though he is a godlike presence in the play who knows the mystery surrounding the Patel family. Being a doctor, he should have been godlike in advising the parents of Tara and Chandan to follow right ethical position in saving lives. He did everything only for boosting his medical achievement through corrupt means.

Characters on stage:

The play is set on a multi-level set. The lowest largest level is the home of the Patels kept only in memory. The second level is the bedsitter of Dan (formerly Chandan) in London, which is the only realistic level in the play. Right at the back on the third level there sits Dr. Thakkar, a god-like commentator.

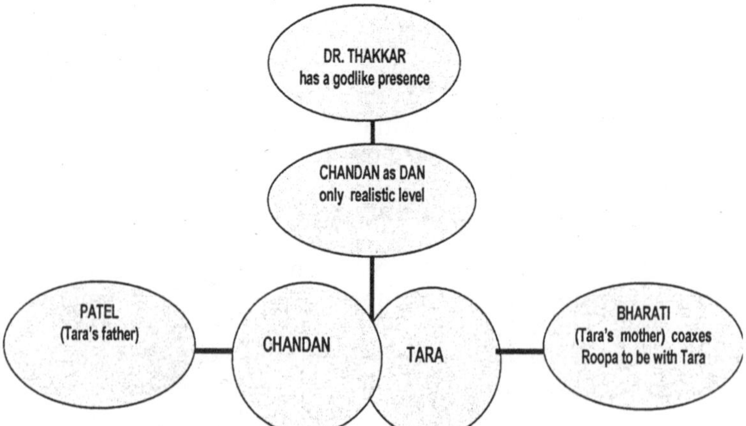

3. The crisis and the quest for atonement

In *Tara* Dattani explores dynamics of familial relationship and the daily emotional turbulence in his characters built on guilt and atonement.

Both Chandan and Tara were physically and emotionally conjoined. Even after their manipulated physical separation. they remain emotionally inseparable throughout. It comes to the knowledge of Tara that it was her mother, in connivance with her grandfather and Dr. Thakkar that decided surgical separation of the conjoined twins. The mental agony that Tara undergoes leads her to waste away her life and succumb to death. Chandan too suffers from bitterness and lives very unhappy. This leads him to change his name to Dan and migrate to London. There, he attempts to recollect the past, writing the story of his life. The play is focused on the psychological exploration of characters. Dan recollects his childhood and attempts to dramatise it through "a series of flashbacks. The play looks at the battles, the victories and the defeats of an Indian family coping with the trauma of freak children and their survival, while also exposing the existing patriarchal stereotypes of the Indian mindset, which has always preferred a boy child to a girl child" (Chaudhuri 37).

It is to be noted that in the Indian tradition, a mother earns her identity through her son as he would be her economic support. It is the son who guarantees performance of the rituals prescribed for salvation (Kakar 2002: 79). In traditional Indian households there is great longing for children. However there is aversion for the girl child. There is indifference to the girl child and her development. This is responsible for the low self-esteem in them. The experience of being not wanted make them secondary to their brothers (Kakar 1988: 48). Indian traditional society being male oriented, creates the gender bias against women. The patriarchal system maintains a male dominated society as the heritage of the family goes to the son and the male members in the family are worshipped. Economically, having a son is considered most important to preserve the family property within the family. A male child is preferred as he is considered to have better opportunities for employment in the labour market. In the patriarchal system it is also a son who brings status and prestige to the family (Dabni 1).

The scene moves to Chandan and Tara who appears limping on stage. Tara speaks out summing up her story. "And me. May be we still are. Like we've always been. Inseparable. The way we started in life. Two lives and one body, in one comfortable womb. Till we were forced out...And separated" (*CP* 325).

Dattani's concept of gender issues depicted in the play leads to "the emergence of the idea of the twin side of one's self – quite literally embodied in one body and the separation that follows" (Chaudhuri 89). The whole story revolves around this mystery of Tara.

Dan is in total confusion as he is trying his hand at writing his story of his long lost sister. Dan introduces the central characters and takes the readers to the beginning of the story when Chandan and Tara were conjoined Siamese kids and the way the surgery was performed to separate them. Central to the story is the gender issue with the preferential treatment of male children. The play is a social criticism on female infanticide in some societies which Dattani puts into the mouth of Roopa who tells Chandan of the rumour she had heard of female infanticide in the Gujarati society.

Apparently the Patels are presented as an ideal couple dedicated to the well being of their handicapped children. But an in-depth analysis reveals manipulations and counter-manipulations and atrocities committed against one another. Though Bharati belonged to a more liberal Kannadiga community, her husband came from a strict patriarchal society. She had no choice but to be subservient to societal demands. Tara reveals the family truths Tara's father had to leave his parents because of the marriage.

Bharati is like any other woman in her social milieu caught up between her choices under societal and familial pressures. Her prejudices are the outcome of her helplessness in an androcentric society. Her sense of guilt drives her to the brink of insanity and hysteria (Choudhuri 718). Bharati turns out to be a split personality in her commitment as a mother and a woman. This is evidenced in her relationship with her son and daughter before and after surgery. She is so very much controlled by societal and familial demands that she is left with "no freewill to assert her own choices" (Agarwal 183) to craft her own destiny. The mistake she makes is that she "continues to be willing instruments in the vicious circle" (Choudhuri 38).

Patel has become a male chauvinist dictating his will in all family matters. However, towards the end when Bharati becomes a neurotic, he tones down in his stand and becomes more caring and accommodating in familial ties. But he never allowed Bharati to confess the truth to Tara seeking atonement for her guilt. She dies in anguish, a neurotic. Tara's stoic courage is very remarkable. Though treated unjustly by the family, she doesn't keep any grudge, but is deeply attached to her brother.

Bharati's guilt drives her to the point of mental break-down. She continues to suffer the qualms of conscience for having denied Tara her leg. Bharati's maternal love for Tara is sacrificed by her surrender to social pressure exerted through her father. She opted for the surgery in favour of Chandan being given the third leg. However, after the surgery when the leg was rejected, her guilt makes her over-protective of Tara, offering her kidney. Bharati is helpless being a victim of patriarchy. She is not even allowed by her husband to confess her guilt and seek forgiveness. Bharati's noble plan does not materialize as her husband does not allow her to do so. Patel turns out to be the antagonist from whose sadistic treatment, Bharati longs to be liberated.

Henceforth, Bharati plays her psychological game becoming over-protective of Tara. She quenches the fire of her sin with love and care and tells Chandan of her plans for Tara: "Yes I plan for her happiness. I mean to give her all love and affection which I can give. It's what she ...deserves. Love can make up for a lot" (*CP* 349). Bharati has her apprehensions about Tara's future when she will mature into an adult: "It's all right while she is young... But let her grow up. Yes, Chandan. The world will tolerate you. The world will accept you – but not her! Oh, the pain she is going to feel when she sees herself at eighteen or twenty. Thirty is unthinkable. And what about forty and fifty! Oh God!" (348-9). Her fears are about societal acceptance of a crippled girl who has no prospects of a decent marriage proposal.

Mr. Patel is a typical patriarch establishing his authority in the family decisions. His male chauvinism is clearly shown when he wants his decisions to be executed regarding the future of his children. He doesn't care for their feelings or plans and dreams. Chandan wants to be a writer while Tara prefers to enter into a profession like her father. While seeing Chandan assist his mother with knitting Patel is annoyed with his wife and his son: "But you can think of turning him into a sissy – teaching him to knit!... I am disappointed in you. From now on you are coming to the office with me. I can't see you rotting at home!" (351).

However, Chandan refuses to do anything without Tara by his side. They continue to be conjoined in fact and spirit as the discussion in the family proves emotionally destructive. Patel keeps asserting himself with regard to all decision making, thereby causing psychological trauma to Bharati and the children. In her existential angst she has to realize the truth of the fact expressed by Simone De Beauvoir that "marriage is the destiny traditionally offered to women by society" (Beauvoir 445). She is defined in her role in her family and Patel exploits it to the full. He further stops his wife making any plans for the children's future. This is a tit-for-tat for her deciding surgery on the children under the influence of her father.

The hidden secret is referred to, namely the way Bharati opted to give the third leg to the boy instead to the girl on whom it would have had better chances of survival. Bharati's guilt makes her over-protective of Tara to compensate her crime. She has virtually become psychologically deranged. Patel wants to rescue her from her mental break-down, which he terms her sickness, and is determined to make all decisions in the family himself. Though, apparently, Patel looks cruel in his remarks, he wants to save the family from more tragedies. He tells Bharati to break out of her own self-absorption and become more sociable. Does he succeed in his plans? Dattani makes his play an excellent means of social criticism, making theatre "a collective experience and the audience have to finish in their own heads what the playwright began" (Nair 10 December) letting the story flow out of Dan's head.

Patel is also shown as a caring husband and father. He looks after Bharati when she is psychologically stressed after the complications of the surgery. "May be I'm expecting the worst... Things are getting out of hand... I must worry about her. Yes. I am worried – about my wife" (*CP* 330). At the same time, he does not allow Bharati to donate her kidney to Tara and has arranged for a donor instead: "Your father's wealth has always been your strength against me…Because I do not want you to have the satisfaction of doing it…. You will have to obey me. It's my turn now" (344). Why does he still victimize her further like a sadist speaking of his turn to take revenge? Knowing her to be a psychiatric case, he still keeps arguing with her to the point of her threatening him to reveal the secret of the past to the children. But Patel is infuriated at this and slaps her saying, "You wouldn't dare tell them. Not you. Please, don't! Not yet!... You cannot tell them. For their sake, don't! If at all they must know, it will be from me. Not from you" (345).

It is a game of revenge that Patel plays, to route everything through his domination in the family. At the same time he doesn't want it to be a shocking experience for the children who would perhaps disregard him for his silence before the unjust surgery. As the father of the family he now wants to give his version of the secret.

There is craving in him to prove to be the ideal father to his children. He tells his daughter, "Tara please believe me when I say that I love you very much and I have never in all my life loved you less or more than I have loved your brother…But your mother would like you to believe that it's not true" (354). He wants by all means to erase the feeling of affection that Tara had developed for her mother, who craved to get Tara emotionally attached to her than to the father. He, instead, is determined to possess her love to establish patriarchal supremacy.

When Tara learns of the surgical manipulation depriving her of a leg being a girl child, she turns bitter towards her mother and utters, "And she calls me her star" (379). She is more bitter due to discrimination. This discovery is a central turning point in the play which "practically kills the female and tears her apart from the male, and Chandan moves far away, never to return, forever incomplete" (Choudhuri 72).

Yet, Tara's behaviour is too mature for a girl of her age, as she keeps her cool in her family relationships. Despite the injustice done to her, she is ever close to her parents, especially to her brother Chandan. She forgets herself thinking of Chandan's future than her own. She tells him, "We women mature fast. Speaking of maturity, you better not skip any physiotherapy sessions. Daddy wants you to be big and sturdy" (*CP* 333). Her angst is expressed when she says, "May be we still are. Like we've always been. Inseparable. The way we started life. Two lives one body, in one comfortable womb. Till we were forced out..." (325).

Chandan and Tara are not only conjoined twins, but they share a unique male-female personality. Chandan presents the male side and Tara, the female side. Together they make a force of love and communion though separately they are weak and dependent. He, on his part, is determined to take care of her future. While discussing Tara's future with his mother he affirms, "Tara is my sister. Everything will be fine" (349). Dan introspects on the injustice meted out to his sister: "She never got a fair deal. Not even from nature. Neither of us did. May be God never wanted us separated. Destiny desires strange things... But even God does not always get what he wants. Conflict is the crux of life" (330). The play ends with Dan making his final apology seeking forgiveness: "Forgive me, Tara. Forgive me for making it my tragedy"(380).

Dan is a victim of angst due to his feeling of guilt associated with the tragedy of Tara. But there is something mutually redeeming in them as there is "the grace of the relationships exist not in their separateness but in their moving in co-ordination or interdependence" (Agarwal 185). When Tara wastes away and dies, Chandan is guilt ridden and escapes to London changing his name to Dan It is an escape mechanism on his part to hide his guilt. But that doesn't help in any way as Tara is a part of himself and she is more than just a sister to him. Mentally and psychologically he continues to be in a state of disillusionment. Guilt ridden he tells his father, "Tara has been dead for six years and Mummy has gone as well, there is nothing left for me to come back to" (*CP* 372).

Finally when the secret is exposed, tragedy strikes in different ways: Tara wastes away and dies. Bharati dies in distress as a psychiatric patient. Patel exists in his own world and Dan in his new 'avatar' attempts to atone for his loss by writing the tragedy of his life.

Dr. Thakkar is like a god-like commentator who narrates to prove his surgical achievement though bribed to perform an unethical surgery. "Tara and Chandan are two sides of the same self rather than two separate entities and that Dan, in trying to write the story of his own childhood, has to write Tara's story. Dan writes Tara's story to rediscover the neglected half of himself, as a means of becoming whole" (Pant 37).

4. Conclusion

It has been pointed out that *Tara* is neither a tragedy of Tara the crippled girl or her brother Chandan, but a tragedy of any society coming to terms with burning issues with its puppet like characters in multiplicity of relationships (Das 57). In the play injustice is meted out not only to Tara, but also to Chandan as he is made a scapegoat. He had no choice but be filled with guilt for the tragedy of Tara for no fault of his, escaping to London. Bharati's heaping love on Tara is an emotional weapon against Patel, besides her seeking atonement, compensating for her part in the crime (Das 55-7).

Dattani's *Tara* is a powerful 'societal reference point' (Jha 26 October) through which he has probed into societal issues kept under carpet due to inbuilt gender prejudices and patriarchal supremacy. The playwright has succeeded in presenting powerfully his social criticism of existing gender discrimination in our society with "active imagination and sense of reality" (Sebastian 28 November 07) and the subsequent guilt and attempt at atonement. It is the socio-cultural system based on gender discrimination that is to blame for the tragedy in the play (Chandra 62). Though everyone tries to seek release from their guilt, the play ends with no final solution in atonement and reconciliation. However, the search for atonement continues throughout on the part of Patel, Bharati and Chandan.

Works Cited

Agarwal, Beena. "Dynamics of Human relationship in Mahesh Dattani's *Tara*." *The Indian Journal of English Studies*. Vol. XLIV, 2007.

Answer.com . *Definition of love.* 2007. http://content.answers.com/main/content/wp/en/thumb/4/42/375px- Love-triangle.jp. Downloaded on 12 June 2009.

Beauvoir, Simone De. *The Second Sex*. Trans. H.M. Parshley. London: Vintage, 1997.

Chaudhuri, Asha Kuthari. *Mahesh Dattani*. New Delhi: Foundation Books, 2005.

Dabni, Jimmy. *Satyadeepam* vol 4-21 October, 2007.

Das, Sangeeta. "Identity Crisis of Women in *Tara*." *The Plays of Mahesh Dattani : A Critical Response*. Ed. R.K. Dhawan & Tanu Pant. New Delhi: Prestige Books, 2005, 51-59.

Chandra, Subhash. "The (Un)twinkling Star: Who Takes Tara's Shine Away?" *The Plays of Mahesh Dattani : A Critical Response*. Ed. R.K. Dhawan & Tanu Pant. New Delhi: Prestige Books, 2005, 60-8.

Dattani, Mahesh. *Collected Plays*. New Delhi: Penguin Books, 2000. (Abbreviated *CP*).

De, Aditi. "Mahesh Dattani's is a voice unafraid to joust with a bleak today." Book Review. *The Hindu*. 7 August 2005. (http://www.hindu.com)

Kakar, Sudhir. *Feminine Identity in India*. New Delhi: Oxford University Press, 1988.

Kakar, Sudhir. *The Indian Psyche*. New Delhi: Oxford University Press, 2002.

Matejcek, Antonín. cited in *Expressionism: Art and Ideas*. Donald E. Gordon, 1987. New Haven: Yale University Press.

Nair, Anita. "The Invisible Observer. " Mahesh Dattani: A Profile. 10 December, 2007. (http://www.anitanair.net)

Pant, Tanu. "Mahesh Dattani: The Face of Indian Drama." *The Plays of Mahesh Dattani : A Critical Response*. Ed. R.K. Dhawan & Tanu Pant. New Delhi: Prestige Books, 2005, 22-50.

Rani, Sudha. On Mahesh Dattani. 10 December 2007. http://www.museindia.com.

Sebastian, A.J. on e-mail correspondence with Mahesh Dattani. 28 November 2007.

Sebastian, A.J, Chandra. *Literary Terms in Drama, Theatre & Cinema*. Delhi: Authorspress. 2002.

—. *Literary Terms in Fiction and Prose*. Delhi: Authorspress. 2004.

Sternberg, Robert. "Triangular theory of love" http://en.wikipedia.org/wiki/Triangular theory_of_love. Downloaded on 13 June 009.

Williams, Tennessee. Glass Menagerie *in Allan G. Halline (Ed.) Six Modern American Plays*. New York: Modern Library, 1963.

3

Patriarchal Subjugation in Mahesh Dattani's "Where There Is A Will"

1. Introduction

In "Where There Is A Will" Mahesh Dattani draws attention to the complexities of relationships under patriarchal hegemony. A patriarch (from Greek: *patria* means father; *arché* means rule, beginning, origin) is a male head of an extended family exercising autocratic authority ("Patriarchy.htm"). Patriarchy is the 'rule of the father'. Within Feminism it refers to 'male domination' in a general sense (Macey 291). Under patriarchy, if a man whose father (and whose father's father, etc.) has died, has two married sons and two married daughters and 15 grandchildren, then any money earned by either of his two sons belongs, not to the individual who earns the money, but to the family, and he, as patriarch of the family, has authority to decide how the money is to be distributed among the family members. He has no similar authority over his married daughters, who are under the authority of the patriarchs of the families into which they have married ("Patriarchy.htm").

According to Allan G. Johnson patriarchal social structures are: (i) Male dominated—which doesn't mean that all men are powerful or all women are powerless—only that the most powerful roles in most sectors of society are held predominantly by men, and the least powerful roles are held predominantly by women (ii) Organized around an obsession with control, with men elevated in the social structure because of their presumed ability to exert control whether rationally or through violence or the threat of violence (iii) Male identified: aspects of society and personal attributes that are highly valued are associated with men, while devalued attributes and social activities are associated with women. There is a sense of threat to the social structure of patriarchies when these gendered associations are destabilized—and the response in patriarchy is to increase the level of control, often by exerting control over women. (iv) Male centered: It is taken for granted that the centre of attention is the natural place for men and boys, and that women should occupy the margins. Public attention is focused on men (Johnson, Allen).

2. Exorcism of the patriarchal code

In *Where There's a Will* Dattani attempts the exorcism of the patriarchal code that subjugates women (*WTW* 451) Hasmukh establishes his patriarchy purely through his wealth sacrificing all familial relationships. His evil designs lead him to have ultimate destructive control over his kith and kin through Kiran, the executrix of his will after death.

Hasmukh Mehta is a self made industrialist who rules his household with an iron hand as an autocratic patriarch. He has final say in everything and has no regard for his wife Sonal, son Ajit or daughter-in-law Preeti. He has no conjugal relationship with Sonal his wife. Ajit, his spendthrift son is frustrated being belittled and ignored by his father. Hasmukh's daughter-in-law Preeti is a scheming character seeking only his money. They are a strange household. Ajit is considered a failure by his father. Hasmukh treats his wife like a servant to keep his house in order. He is suspicious of daughter-in-law Preeti's intelligence. She is the only one who can match his lack of concern for any one. Hasmukh heads such a family and keeps everyone under his patriarchal control.

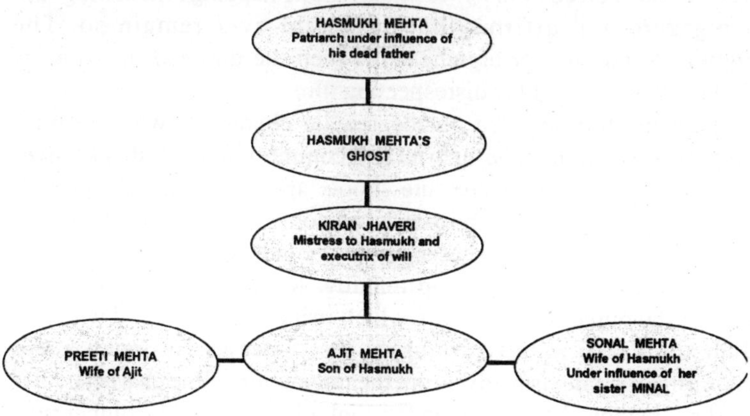

As the play opens Ajit is on the phone talking to a friend about his frustration as his father does not give him Rs. 5 Lakhs to modernize the factory. Being the company's JMD, he has plans to diversify the business to manufacture electronic typewriters. As the telephonic conversation continues, his father Hasmukh keeps commenting on Ajit's irresponsible and crackpot schemes (455). He goes to the extent of cursing the day Ajit was born and wishes him dead. There is comical irony in his utterance:

> ...I actually prayed to get him. Oh God! I regret it all. Please let him drop dead. No, no. What a terrible thing to say about one's own son. I take it back. Dear God, don't let him drop dead. Just turn him into a nice vegetable so he won't be in my way. Ever since he entered my factory, he has been in my way (455).

Confrontation between Hesmukh and his son Ajit ensues as the father considers Ajit a bankrupt twenty-three year old wastrel. However, Ajit claims to be brainy and young blooded, though inexperienced. He is confident that with his talent and vigour he can contribute to the company's growth. The more he claims his right to prove his worth, Ajit is taunted by his father as a good for nothing saying, "I am not trying to humiliate you. I am trying to put some sense into you. Trying to fill up empty space" (458). Ajit exposes his father's selfish motives due to depravity in childhood. "Anything I do is wrong for you! Just because you are a self-made man and had a deprived childhood... Nothing I do will ever seem intelligent to you. You are prejudiced" (459). Hasmukh keeps nagging Ajit calling him a big zero and affirms that he would ever remain so. The argument and counter argument between the duo end up with the father slapping Ajit for disrespecting him.

Dattani focuses also on the female characters who are busy preparing for dinner. The quarrel and commotion send shock waves to Sonal as her blood pressure shoots up. Still she busies herself preparing dishes for her husband and son. She is like a machine churning out the same dishes as usual – salad which Hasmukh never eats. Still she refuses to stop making. Ironically she also makes orange flavoured halva for Ajit which irritates her husband who is a diabetic. Preeti is busy arranging the plates as Hasmukh keeps enquiring if dinner is ready. From the interaction of the characters it is evident that they have no deep familial relationship. The dinner time is only a daily ritual of bonding. Each one is suspicious of the other – the only unifying factor is the wealth of Hasmukh which they long to inherit after his death. The dinner table brings them all together and Hasmukh continues his tirade against Ajit and utters, "You should get a son like yourself. He will finish you off much faster than you've finished me" (463).

As Hasmukh retires to his room he regrets having had Ajit got married at a young age. He reminisces with complacency his patriarchal supremacy inherited from his father. "I am forty-five and look at what I have achieved. This is because I had the good sense to learn from my father" (463). Unlike his wayward brother who roamed about the streets singing praises of Lord Krishna, Hasmukh was forced to work hard dreaming of becoming a millionaire. Tragedy struck with his early marriage to Sonal and the early birth of Ajit. Despite it all he was able to build a business empire, becoming one of the richest business tycoons. He regrets that his son Ajit on the contrary is on his road to failure at twenty-three. The bitter argument between Hasmukh and Ajit leads the latter to drive off to be with his friends.

Hasmukh continues to reveal his frustration after his son took over the business. He also makes detesting remarks on Sonal his wife with whom he never enjoyed marital bliss. "Twenty-five years of marriage and I don't think she has ever enjoyed sex.... And I haven't enjoyed sex with her" (473). Frustrated in his conjugal life he began his affair with Kiran Jhaveri, his typist and secretary, in whom he found brains that matched his.

The scene comically shifts to Sonal conversing with Preeti as she clears the dinner table. Sonal ironically comments on the meaning of 'Hasmukh' which means 'a smiling face'. But her husband never smiled, blaming her and her son for all his problems. She reveals how Hasmukh had lost his mother when he was only four. He married only to fill the vacuum of a woman in his life as he utters:

> Why does a man marry? So that he can have a woman to himself? No. There's more to it than that. What? May be he needs a faithful companion? No. If that was it, all men would keep dogs. No. No, I think the important reason anyone should marry at all is to get a son. Why is it so important to get a son? Because the son will carry on the family name? Why did I marry? Yes, to get a son. So that when I grow old, I can live life again through

> my son. Why did my father marry? To get me. Why did I marry? To get Ajit ...Then I should be a very happy man. I've got a loving wife who has been faithful to me like any dog would be. She has given me a son....I should be happy.... I've got what I want... Why do I have a mistress? Because I am unhappy... Why am I unhappy? Because I don't have a son. Who is Ajit...He's just a boy who spends my money and lives in my house... He doesn't behave like my son. A son should make me happy. Like I made my father... happy. That is what I wanted my son to make me...But he failed! Miserably! He has not a single quality I look for in a son...It won't be long before everything I worked for and achieved will be destroyed! (474-5).

In the second part of the play, the scene shifts to Hasmukh's death. He rises from his bed and observes his corpse. He moves behind the bed and speaks calmly of his death. Applying magic realism, Dattani has very deftly brought in the scene to establish the protagonist's patriarchal hegemony even after death. "I am dead. I can see my own body lying still on the bed. Looking peaceful, but dead" (476). The ghost of Hasmukh makes comments throughout the rest of the play adding much humour to the sequences.

Act I scene ii takes the story a week after his death. Lying on the sofa, Hasmukh makes a weekly round up of events. He feels good to be dead since it has put an end to his health problems. "No more kidney problems, no backaches, no irregular heartbeats, no heartbeats" (479). But the family was bothered with too many condolence phone calls, rush of visitors and the paraphernalia of the funeral. The gathering was very impressive as family friends kept pouring into the bedroom to pay their last respects to the departed. His wife kept up her appearance of great loss crying at the appropriate moments under instructions from Minal. Hasmukh struck even headlines in the media. He felt good knowing how famous he was after death with obituary in the papers full of photographs inserted by his own different companies. The ironic way the dead man continues to wield his patriarchy is noteworthy. "Now it's all over. My life is over and I have no business hanging around here. I should be flying to heaven on a buffalo. But what about the mess that's down here? What about all my money?... I don't think they deserve all that money. None of them have worked for it, especially not my son... You see, I have made a special will! They are going to hate me for doing this to them!" (479).

In the sequence that follows, the family arrives home from the solicitor's office. They have been summoned by the solicitor as per Hasmukh's will and testament. They are all very upset after having learnt about the will by which he has ruined them all. They begin their bickering and quarrelling over the turn of events, accusing each other for Hasmukh making them suffer. Preeti accuses Ajit for bringing out the disaster on all of them by his not being nice to his father. The trio keep accusing each other for the ugly turn of events. The only remedy left is to put their heads together for a final solution:

> AJIT: ...Now we can't contest the will. It was all his money and his property. He could do whatever he liked with it.
>
> SONAL: But why did he do this to us? He must have been mad!
>
> PREETI: Mad! That's it! We can say that he wasn't in the right frame of mind when he made the will. We'll get certificates to prove he was senile! (482).

But their plan doesn't work as Ajit recalls how his father had a qualified physician as witness while executing his will, who had attached a certificate stating his sound mind while signing the document.

Meanwhile Sonal's sister Minal calls to enquire of the legal developments after Hasmukh's death. It is to be noted that Minal wields great influence over Sonal which Hasmukh always resented. Ajit tells Minal how things have become bad for them as his father has formed Hasmukh Mehta Charitable trust to deal with all his property, finances and shares including the house where they live. They are all to receive a regular allowance from the trust. The will states that the trust would continue to direct Ajit until he turns forty five. A certain Kiran Jhaveri, Hasmukh's mistress, is named executrix of the will. Ajit begins to reflect on his misery and expresses his bitterness as he talks:

> You must be happy now, wherever you are. Ever since I was a little boy you have been running my life. Do this, do that or don't do that, do this... Then, when I grew up, I learnt to answer

> you back. I think it was worth disagreeing with you. At least I have the satisfaction of knowing that you were worried about me (487).

The scene that follows opens with a comical note with Hasmukh making comments on his garlanded photograph. He is upset since they have not kept fresh flowers just as he used to do for his father's larger photograph. He finds the picture not up to his expectations being faulty at the cheeks, lips and eyes. He reminisces how he had locked up his father's photograph after honouring it for some time. Similarly, his own photograph will be dumped by his son some day. He has premonition that he will meet the same fate in the future when everyone would forget his memory. Frustrated the ghost of Hasmukh decides on a ghostly action: "I think I'll go outside and swing on the tamarind tree. Upside down" (488).

Act II scene i ends with the arrival of Kiran, Hasmukh's mistress, who has come to stay in the house being named the executrix of the will. The role assigned to Kiran is similar to that of Oedipa Maas in Thomas Pynchon's *The Crying of Lot 49*, where she receives a letter naming her the legal executrix of the estate of Pierce Inverarity, one of her wealthy ex-boyfriends. She knows that the estate was in total mess, however, Oedipa silently resolves to perform her duty. She suspects that her husband, Mucho Maas, will not be able to give her any help. "The letter was from the law firm of Warpe…, and signed by somebody named Metzger. It said Pierce had died back in the spring, and they'd only just now found the will… Oedipa had been named also to execute the will in a codicil dated a year ago" (Pynchon 2). Similarly, Kiran is appointed the executrix of Hasmukh's will. Both the women are mistresses to the men involved and are forced by circumstances to leave their legal husbands.

The focus of attention is Kiran and the way the other characters show their displeasure in having her in the house. She makes it very clear that she prefers to stay in the house than in her flat. Ajit, Preeti and Sonal lambast her with queries on her affair with Hasmukh. She goes on to reveal how Hasmukh got her married to a man whom she supplied booze to be drowned in it to be mistress to Hasmukh. It was her intellectual acumen that attracted Hasmukh in his passionless marriage. Kiran establishes her indispensability as she has come to assist them as per Hasmukh's will.

Preeti sums up the shame faced by the family: "The will has left us all naked. The whole world is saying, 'Hasmukh Mehta didn't have faith in his own family. He didn't get along with his wife. His son is a spendthrift. His daughter-in-law is a scheming little witch. That's why he left all his wealth in the hands of an outsider' " (*WTW* 493).

Kiran, however, side tracks their accusations of having influenced Hasmukh to become his mistress and clears their misunderstanding about her authority. "I am only the trustee of all his wealth. Not the owner...Everything rightfully belongs to the three of you. Provided you follow his instructions" (493). She asserts that Ajit will be briefed to attend daily to his duties and the two women will be given their regular maintenance allowance. The trust will be automatically dissolved when Ajit's child would be twenty-one and Ajit would be made the heir to the property. Kiran's duty is to train Ajit and eventually delegate the responsibilities to him. Meanwhile she would leave her husband and be in the Hasmukh household. When they protest at the deal, Kiran warns them of the consequences that "the holdings of the trust will be divided between certain charitable institutions recommended by the founder" (494). Cursing Hasmukh's evil machinations, the family relents to the proposal of Kiran.

Act II scene ii opens with a comical sequence where Hasmukh sits on the dining table cross-legged, commenting on the grim family situations. He talks to the audience about his perception of life after death and demonstrates how to lie upside down from a tamarind tree to observe his family:

> Have you ever swung on a tamarind tree? Upside down?... You can see the world the way it really is...That's the way I see my family now. Their lives have been turned upside down since Kiran entered this house...You may ask – what kind of a fool would ask his mistress to live with his family? A fool who knows his family very well. Kiran may have been my mistress, but she has far more brains than my wife! Transformed. From stupid incapable housewife to clever incapable housewife. Every day is a new lesson for her on husband-understanding. The more time she spends with Kiran, the more she learns about me. The more she learns about me, the more she'll regret having been such a good-for-nothing wife. That will keep her from being a happy widow ever after...... I want Kiran here. To keep a check on mydaughter-in-law (496).

His intentions are very clear – to prevent any happiness to any of his family members after death, thereby exercising perfect patriarchal hegemony. Things have turned out to be very difficult for Ajit who feels frustrated after the first day in office under the strict formalities executed by Kiran. Sympathizing with his sorry plight, the mother consoles him saying that he has to patiently endure the ordeal for twenty-one years. The ghost of Hasmukh blames his wife for bringing up Ajit like an irresponsible baby. Meanwhile the briefcase he carelessly keeps on the bed hurts Preeti who lands on it, hurting her tummy. She is enraged:

> PREETI: What have you done, you lout? What if something happens to the baby?
> AJIT: Oh, no! Don't say that!
> HASMUKH: If anything goes wrong, I'll never forgive you! (499).

Hasmukh's reaction is typical of establishing his patriarchal supremacy. He longs to have sway over everything in his household including his grandchild to be born. Preeti cannot bear any more the ordeal of being haunted by the will of Hasmukh being executed by his mistress. She longs to exorcise the ghost of Hasmukh, but utters her helplessness: "A picture of a perfect family. The widowed mother, the expectant mother, the son who has stepped into his late father's shoes without a peep, and of course the mistress of the house. The only one left to complete the picture in your father" (500). Ajit bitterly acknowledges that he was forced to step into his father's shoes, being shoved into it. All are equally upset over the ghost of Hasmukh continuing to dictate terms through the will:

> AJIT: He is still alive. Through his will! Through his mistress!
>
> PREETI: Oh! The two things I hate most in this house. The will and his mistress! Followed closely by your mother.
>
> AJIT: He is making me do things he wanted me to do. Through her! In the office. Without realizing it, she has replaced father and is replacing me with father….Everything she tells me to do is exactly what he would have wanted me to do. We are all living out a dead man's dream!.... I can't fight him now. He has won. He has won because he's dead. But when he was alive, I

> did protest. In my own way. Yes, I'm happy I did that. Yes, I did fight back. I did do 'peep peep' to him! That was my little victory (501).

Preeti, on the other hand, was more intelligent and scheming in handling Hasmukh. She had warned Ajit to endure his father's bossy nature. However, he didn't relent, instead always retorted in justification. On her part she simply relented to his exerting authority "I gave in, I simply listened to him and didn't 'protest' like you! I knew he didn't have long to live. I thought, why not humour him for a few days! After he's gone, we can have all the freedom to do what we want, and also all the money. I almost succeeded. He would have left everything to us if you hadn't 'protested'. That was your mistake!" (501-2). Being a scheming woman, she had planned it intelligently even by mixing her vitamin tablets with Hasmukh's medicines in the same bottle. She blamed Ajit for having made her and her future child paupers by his habit of answering back his father. Meanwhile, searching for her Calmpose tablets, Ajit finds the medicine bottle with vitamin and other tablets.

The scene shifts to the conversation between Sonal and Kiran. Sonal is surprised to know how Kiran manages all her household chores and attend to her office diligently. Kiran takes pride in managing everything on her own including her husband which drew the attention of Hasmukh to make her the executrix of his will. Sonal accuses her of having an affair with her husband. But Kiran has her thought out answer: "Mrs Mehta, no woman has an affair with an older man, especially a married man, for a little bit of respect and trust. It was mainly for money" (506). Kiran's honest confession makes the two women come closer in understanding. Now, Sonal's complaints are about her daughter-in-law who has become a menace to her for the sake of money. Kiran advices Sonal to look at the turn of events from a different perspective. She is told to see Preeti's actions ruled by circumstances to make money. When Kiran tells that it is more important to give than to receive, Sonal declarers that she never got because she never gave. At this the ghost of Hasmukh feels fulfilled in his plans as his wife has learnt the lesson, and he can go to heaven and Kiran back home.

The conversation between the two women further leads to Kiran's speaking' of her family and the way her mother was ill treated by her alcoholic father. She and her brothers had grown up seeing their mother endure their drunken father beat her. "I learnt what life was when my mother pretended she was happy in front of me and my brothers, so that we wouldn't hate my father" 508). To keep her mother away from her father, Kiran got him fully drunk daily, so that he would sleep off at the dining table and would be too drunk to harm any one. She learnt her lesson from life that men "were weak men with false strength" (508). This is a revelation to Sonal who is told how mean and weak her husband was:

> Hasmukh was intoxicated with his power. He thought he was invisible. That he could rule from his grave by making this will... Isn't it strange how repetitive life is? My brothers. They have turned out to be like their father, going home with bottles of rum wrapped up in newspapers. Beating up their wives. And I – I too am like my mother. I married a drunkard...And I too have learnt to suffer silently. Oh! Where will all this end? Will the scars our parents lay on us remain for ever? (508).

Kiran's reference to "scars" of parents remaining for ever is similar to what Mrs Alving utters in Ibsen's *Ghost:*

> Ghosts... we are all ghosts...there is in me something ghostlike from which I can never free myself... It isn't just what we have inherited from our father and mother that walks in us. It is all kind of dead ideas and all sorts of old and obsolete beliefs. They are not alive in us; but they remain in us none the less, and we can never rid ourselves of them (Ibsen 39).

Scars and ghosts of lingering patriarchal hegemony need be ostracised, if life has to go on for the living in both the plays.

Kiran's disclosures bring all the character in the Hasmukh household united in action with the executrix to get them all out of the claws of the will. Kiran also reveals how Ajit lived all the time in the shadows of his father having no independent life of his own, devoid of his own dreams. Everything was planned for him by Hasmukh, treating him exactly the way Hasmukh's own father had treated him. Kiran further reveals the mental trauma Hasmukh suffered: "He depended on me for everything. He thought he was the decision maker. But I was. He wanted me to rule his life. Like his father had. Hasmukh didn't really want a mistress. He wanted a father. He saw in me a woman who would father him!...Men never really grow up!" (*WTW* 510).

Kiran felt disgust for Hasmukh and hated him like her own father, brothers and husband. She felt pity for them as Hasmukh continued to rule over them even after death through his will. He did all that only to continue in his father's foot steps who ruled his family with an iron hand. She was glad that Ajit by revolting against his father, had escaped from the scars and ghosts of the past: "He may not be the greatest rebel on earth, but at least he is free of his father's beliefs. He resists...That is enough to prove that Ajit has won and Hasmukh has lost" (510).

The revelations bring Hasmukh household together in their fight against the ghost of Hasmukh. As the scene of reconciliation between Kiran and the others take place, the ghost of Hasmukh grows more and more panicky as his evil designs are defeated. The household is so happy with Kiran that they invite her to stay with them for ever. The ghost realizes his own folly being ruled by his own father's patriarchy all his life:

> HASMUKH: It is ...true? Have I merely been to my father what Ajit has been to me? Have all my achievements been my father's aspirations for me? Have I been my father's ghost? If that is true, then where was I? What became of me, the real me? (511).

Kiran's explanations open the eyes of Sonal to stand on her own feet, rejecting the aid of her sister Minal under whose shadow she lived all the time. She had to break loose from ghosts of her own making in her stressful life under her husband.

Kiran also finds how Hasmukh had a slow lingering death consuming wrong tablets for his ailments. Preeti had mixed her vitamin tablets along with his medicines. All the tablets in the bottle looked alike apparently. After Hasmukh's death Preeti had hidden the medicine bottle making excuses that she didn't need them any more. Kiran, however, questions Preeti on the matter while she trembles and begins to sob:

> The tablets you threw out of the window were the ones for his high blood pressure. The tablets I found on his dressing table

> were your… vitamins. When did you exchange them? Oh, you could have done it any time. You had plenty of opportunity. He was right – you are very clever. Of course you didn't kill him. You just let nature do the work for you. Were you so impatient? Couldn't you wait a few more years? Oh, I'm glad he made this will! You don't deserve any of his money (513).

Though Preeti is cornered there is no definite proof for the accusation levelled against her. Kiran can't go to the police either lacking clear evidence. Although Kiran has the power to disinherit Preeti, she didn't want to do it for the sake of Ajit and the child to be born. Instead, she plans of letting Ajit know facts, thus inciting in him hatred for his wife. Since Preeti pleads Kiran not to tell it all to Ajit, she desists and changes the topic of conversation to the surprise birthday party Preeti has planned for Ajit.

As the party progresses, they all decide to be good friends for the rest of the twenty-one years as per the clause in the will. Their hearty cheering drives Hasmukh's ghost out of the house. He runs to stay permanently on the tamarind tree outside, regretting for having made the will, which ultimately drove him out. The conversation shifts to Sonal, expressing the neighbours' concern about the tamarind tree, obstructing their electric wires. Ajit decides to cut it off as soon as his servant returned. Meanwhile Preeti experiences her baby move in her womb, as if suddenly sprung into life. The cutting of the tamarind tree will drive Hasmukh's ghost out of his shelter for ever, ending the patriarchal hegemony. Sonal also decides to break with her past from the shadows of her sister Minal by firmly responding to her over telephone, "…as far as I'm concerned you can jump into a bottomless pit!" (516).

By trying to establish supreme control over his family through his money and will, Hasmukh was only perpetrating the filthy tradition inherited from his father. Somewhere the hegemony had to stop. Ajit revolts against patriarchy and establishes his final victory. At the end, they all join hands being victims of the same male domination and ruthless patriarchy. Dattani has successfully explored like Ibsen some of the problems faced by patriarchal societies that need purging of the ghosts of the past.

3. Multiplicity of relationships

"Where There's a Will" is a superb study on human relationships. It is very strange that the familial relationships in Hasmukh household is basically one of non-love as patriarchy rules with an iron hand. Hesmukh treats his son as a zero indicative of psychological break-down in his own life having been a victim of patriarchy himself. Therefore he fights the ghosts of patriarchy by perpetrating the same evil, fulfilling the adage 'father like son.' Since Ajit has the guts to challenge his father, he is crushed economically, disregarding any feelings of closeness, connectedness, and bondedness by Hasmukh.

Hasmukh's relationship with his wife is frigid empty love. There is no intimacy in relationship and he goes on with his extra-marital affair with Kiran. Sonal on her part merely fulfils the roles as wife mechanically all the time. She also allows herself to be under the perpetual shadow of her sister Minal.

Hasmuk's love for Kiran is only from infatuation as he needed a mother and mistress in her. On her part Kiran found Hasmukh a growing up child who needed psychological mothering from her. She hated him finding in him a replica of her father, brothers and husband. But she used him to amass wealth for herself.

Relationship betweem Ajit and Preeti remains merely at the level of companionate love as she married him only for his money. On his part, Ajit needed a woman merely as a companion in his life-long fight against patriarchy. As the play ends companionate love relationship is built between Kiran, Ajit, Sonal and Preeti to fight the ghost of Hasmukh.

4. Conclusion

"Where There's a Will" while examining familial relationships, centres on exorcising patriarchy that continues to wreck bliss in family life. At the bottom of it all, it is psychological depravity that leads Hasmukh to exercise his supreme authority – belittling his son, wife and daughter-in-law. Finding no positive qualities in any of his relations, he searches for fulfilment and psychological bliss in extra-marital relationship. Finally he is crushed by his own machinations. Dattani's ideas consolidate to expose social evils that continue to fester in our social net-working. Ajit finally has been able to expose his father's follies by his timely revolt to escape from scars of the past.

Dattani has deftly drawn attention to issues seldom discussed, with humour and irony, calling for social introspection. Though written in the backdrop of a Gujarati family, "Where There's a Will" is applicable to joint-family system prevalent in several parts of India. The patriarchal control is examined in two parts: in life and in death. In life Hasmukh haunted his family daily with his autocratic control. The bickering in the household escalates with the death of Hasmukh, when the ghost of the dead man, keeps his sway over with the execution of the will. In the final analysis, when all stand united, the sins of the forebears are rooted out when Hasmukh's ghost is driven out with the cutting of the tamarind tree. Kiran's assessment of extreme patriarchal control in Hasmukh as a substitute for his inadequacy as a man, finally resolves the conflict among the characters and brings them together to derive benefit from the Hasmukh will.

Works Cited

Dattani, Mahesh. "Where There's a Will." *Collected Plays.* New Delhi: Penguin Books, 2000, pp.450-516. (Abbreviated *WTW*).

Ibsen, Henrik. *Ghosts*. Madras: Macmillan India Limited, 1989.

Johnson, Allen.ghttp://gray.intrasun.tcnj.edu/Coming%20of%20Age/a_basic_definition_of_patriarchy.htm

Macey, David. *The Penguin Dictionary of Critical Theory*. London: Penguin, 2000.

"Patriarch.htm", httpa://www.economicexpert.com.

Pynchon, Thomas. *The Crying of Lot 49*. New York: Perennial Classics, 1999.

4

Existential Working of Human mind in Vijay Tendulkar's *The Cyclewallah* (*The Cyclist*)

Vijay Tendulkar (1828-2008), in his multi-faceted career as a journalist, novelist and essayist has authored in the last fifty years, thirty two full-length plays, twenty five one-act plays, six collections of children's plays, four collections of short stories, three collections of essays, seventeen film scripts and a novel. Written in Marathi, his plays have been translated into English and other languages, and have been performed the world over. Known also as a social activist, he has dwelt on social themes.

This paper attempts to explore the existential working of human mind in *The Cyclewallah* (1992). (*The Cyclist*)

Existentialist doctrines purport that man is continually confronted with varied possibilities among which he may choose and through which he can project his life. He is puzzled by the dread of death, the struggle and suffering of daily life. He finds his life absurd as it dangles between his infinite aspirations and finite possibilities. According to Kierkegaard 'Human existence is irremediably finite; it's standpoint is incorrigibly partial and limited' (Emmanuel 61). Man is thus cornered by angst (dread) which is 'a sympathetic antipathy and an antipathetic sympathy' (Kierkegaard 42). It is very relevant here to ponder over possibility and reality in Existentialist viewpoint:

> He who is educated by dread is educated by possibility, and only the man who is educated by possibility is educated in accordance with his infinity. Possibility is therefore the heaviest of all categories...When such a person, therefore, goes out of the school of possibility, and knows more thoroughly than a child knows the alphabet that he can demand of life absolutely nothing, and the terror, perdition, annihilation, dwell next door

> to every man, and has learned the profitable lesson that every dread which alarms (aengste) may the next instant become a fact, he will then interpret reality differently, he will extol reality, and even when it rests upon him heavily he will remember that after all it is far, far lighter than the possibility was (Friedman 370-71).

It is this existential human predicament that Tendulkar presents in *The Cyclist.* The play evidently shows the influence of the theatre of the absurd, 'characterised by illogical situations, unconventional dialogue, and minimal plots to express the apparent absurdity of human existence and metaphysical anguish' (Sebastian 14). The dramatist concerns himself with the doomed individual, the man in despair and distress, alone and bitter in the wide world. For him reality is meaningless and senseless. Man has to face it in all its senselessness and should have the courage to laugh at it. The true field of battle is inside us, in the Unconscious. An absurdist confronts the audience with harsh facts of isolated life in an alien world. In the tradition of the absurdists the playwright presents the similarity of human nature through an allegory:

> The cyclewallah is a reflection of people who spend their entire lives in a fantasy without any understanding of reality. But to live in the true sense of the word, a person must live through situations that force him to look beyond himself, situations which shock him by confronting him with the unimaginable,' says Tendulkar. Perhaps it is this hard-hitting impact of Tendulkar's plays, which jolts audiences out of their complacency each time that accounts, more than any other element, for their immortality (Bahadur).

Summing up his weltanschauung of life portrayed in his plays, he considers life as an inescapable challenge:

> 'I personally don't bother about people who haven't seen life. They close their eyes at the sight of suffering as if it doesn't exist. The fact is that life is dark and cruel, it's just that you don't care for the truth. You don't want to see it because it might make you uncomfortable. If escapism is your way of living then you will fail to see the truth. I have not written about hypothetical pain or created an imaginary world of sorrow. I am from a middle

> class family and I have seen the brutal ways of life by keeping my eyes open. My work has come from within me, as an outcome of my observation of the world in which I live. (Abjijeet).

The play is central to all his writings like an 'ultimate comment on himself and the reality surrounding him' (Tendulkar vii) in an allegorical manner as in the 20th century 'Expressionist Drama' and 'Theatre of the Absurd.' Through episodic structure, Tendulkar has also recourse to Naturalism which rejects free will in man and believes that human behaviour is controlled by instinct, emotion, or social and economic factors. Man is a passive victim of natural forces (Sebastian 157). The playwright concentrates on the states of mind and human situations and confronts the audience with harsh facts of isolated life in an alien world.

The play examines the mental journey of the protagonist who is beset with the basic existential problem of the meaning of life and truth. It is an excellent matter for societal criticism. The dramatist had very succinctly compared the absurd situation of the play to the situation of India at the turn of the new millennium saying: 'Life here is as in *The Cyclist,* It will never change' (Tendulkar xii). The play however remains very enigmatic to the readers/audience with its multi-faceted sequence of events.

As the stage brightens the audience is given a strange sight of an object covered with a white sheet. The protagonist, a cyclist eager to begin a tour uncovers the object, an exercise wheelless bicycle. He is a Prufrock type of a character who is lean with thinning hair. Wearing garments borrowed from friends, he looks comical with a backpack, cap, and sunglasses. He is eager to begin his expedition and checks the bicycle, pedalling back and forth. A banner 'Expedition/Trip 200- ' is placed on the handle.

The first sequence begins with the Main Character making a mental checklist and explains to the audience the nature of his trip which has symbolic significance. It is a journey both geographical and psychological with allusions to the history of the bicycle.

> The Xs... three Xs. Each refers to the type of trip I have in mind. A geographical journey – across an island, a sub-continent, a continent, across the ocean. Or a journey of the mind, or just a bicycle trip... My dream voyage is about to be fulfilled! I am

> thrilled. Many years ago, I had dreamt this dream... that ....I should pick up a cycle, the bicycle. Get on it and ride. See unexplored places – mountains, deserts, water...The voyage is ready to take off.(Tendulkar 6-7).

He is all set and plays a popular tune on his harmonica. Suddenly he stops the music as he is scared of an unknown fear that grips him. He has never been out on such an expedition as his Amma and Pa never let him out of home being the only child. He was walled within his home over-protected by his parents. He played inside the house on his tricycle. By and by he began to build his dream of cycling out into the world: 'I am on the landing, near the stairs. I ride down the stairs. Then I can see the road outside our front door. And in the distance, the bridge across the rail tracks, and running along the bridge, the highway! There, I am standing proud over my bicycle' (8).

The various episodes/sequenceslead the Main Character through his allegorical journey whereby he encounters Amma (Ma), Pa (Papa), Man (Jogeshtey Uncle), Passer-by, Sage, Crowd (A,B,C, and Z), First (Lord of the Earth), Second (Lord of Heavens), Bandit, Lion, Figure (Ghost), and Woman (Mermaid).

1. In the first sequence the Main Character finds his Pa and Amma raising objections to his expedition warning him of the dangers and violence brewing everywhere in the form of various threats presented like an absurd chain in a disturbed mind: Kidnapping - Tigers – Naxalites -corrupt politicians – deserts – canyons - mountains – Talibans – floods – earthquake – drugs – AIDS. Whatever be the consequences he is determined to pursue his dream, lest he regrets of it later in life. Pa and Amma bid him farewell with parental warnings: 'Go if you must. But don't fall off the bike. Don't go on the highways...Go. You know the signs? Stop, Yield, Go...Meet politicians. Keep away from them...See how difficult it is to let you go' (10). Bidding them goodbye he pedals off enthusiastically chasing his dream.
2. While ringing his bicycle bell in jubilation he rings the imaginary door bell of Man (Jogeshtey Uncle) who shows his annoyance.
3. As he rides on, the Main Character finds three roads coming up. mistakes in his choice.

MAIN CHARACTER: But there are three roads.
PASSER-BY: Drop dead! Who has a three-sided coin? Stay here. Don't go anywhere.
MAIN CHARACTER: Impossible! I've left on a world tour and you say I
shouldn't go anywhere? You're ruining my trip. Same as Pa and Amma (13).

Despite the discouraging suggestions given, the Cyclist makes his decision to go on his journey commenting, 'You come across all types, that's what Pa said... I didn't want to listen... then I thought, why worry, who has time!' (13). The sequence has a digression as the Main Character briefly recounts the history of bicycle.

4. The next sequence brings the protagonist interacting with a Sage who is on a trip to America on foot claiming it to be more reliable. The Main Character realises he has not pedalled at all. When he asks, 'Where did I come from? he is told by the Sage 'From your mother's womb' (15). Mounting his bicycle he keeps pedalling.
5. He recounts how Kirpatrick the blacksmith who invented the first bike accidentally hit a child. The Main Character becomes everyman representing Kirpatrick who is surrounded by a crowd for having run over and killed a Murgi. He pleads for mercy: 'But I...I'm a vegetarian – Murgis, chickens, rabbits, cows – I don't eat – why would I kill...' (17). He is asked to pay one hundred rupees as fine for the Murgi, and is told 'your Pa killed it!' Back on his bike, he rides on narrating the story of Kirkpatrick who run over a child.
6. Next he meets the First (Lord of the Earth) and the Second (Lord of Heavens). The two Lords decide to file a case against the protagonist for trespassing into their territory. He however tries to excuse himself and to pursue his world tour since he stepped on their property unknowingly. The two Lords meanwhile quarrel over their territorial supremacy leading to a cosmic fight. In wonderment The Cyclist recalls what his Pa told him, '...there's nothing free any more. Air, water, even the sunset

– has to be paid for, permission sought. Only a bicycle trip is cheap' (21).

7. The Bandit episode that ensues brings to focus the argument between the two over the burglar alarm by which the protagonist is warned of invading robbers. The Bandit is determined to rob the alarm from the Main Character who in turn is willing to part with a camera that snaps pictures of feelings and emotions. He further adds, 'When you get tired of the shotgun, you can shoot people with the camera' (23).
8. When the roaring Lion approaches, the main character thinks it to be the sound of gas in his stomach. In the blinding darkness he strokes the lion and expresses his great regret : 'If he ate me up then… wouldn't be able to continue this world trip…' Meanwhile the cyclist boasts of his assuming the role as a Superman or Tarzan. The Lion responds by narrating how he ate up Tarzan and retired for a sieta in the cave. He thinks of eating up the cyclist but refrains as, 'There's hardly any meat on him – no fun eating him. He'll only stick in my craw' (26).
9. The sequence is interrupted by the Main Character determined to write his travel diary, capturing the events of the day like any great traveller. 'This morning, exactly seven-twenty… left on journey… Amma, Pa, farewells… Three paths… fat Murgi… Turkey… Bandit… Trespass… Lords of Earth and Heavens… Lion…' (27).
10. In the meantime a Figure appears warning the Main Character of a Ghost sitting next to him. The Figure tells him to die and become a ghost. The Figure recounts the story of his previous lives as a successful businessman and later re-incarnated as a politician. He faked shooting himself and became a ghost of an actor-politician. When the figure reveals himself as a ghost and challenges the main character to wrestle with him, he cries for help from Pa.
11. In the sequence that follows Pa appears in divine light advising him how to exorcize the ghost by patience and setting his thoughts, words and deeds in unison. Pa also warns him to be on his guard and to maintain courage.

    PA: Nothing! On such occasions, the best solution is to do nothing.

MAIN CHARACTER: Nothing?

PA: In this life, the worst possible tragedies happen – individually, nationally, globally – these occur, and their solution: DO NOTHING. Every problem ultimately resolves itself... In the end, nothing will happen. That's the secret. Follow this, and the victory will be yours! (31).

12. As the Main Character struggles with the Figure he hears the sound of a cock crowing ending the ghost's night. He is delighted to scribble his diary as the first night of his dramatic adventure ends. He is determined never to turn back but to continue forward to see the whole world. Meanwhile a thunder rages and he is drenched in water and finds it impossible to pedal on. In his unabated determination he forges ahead saying, ' Gone! The thunder, the lightning, the rain gone!! Man can't be destroyed. No one can destroy my will to complete my journey! Nature must submit. Pa, you didn't say anything about Nature, but your son figured it out all...' (33). He then hangs all his rain-soaked clothes one by one on a rope - shirt, trousers and underwear. Feeling himself so light like in childhood, he limps around in joy and wonderment having, 'no worries about clothes... let the clothes dry then I'm ready to move – with a new spirit, a new resolve... Such ease. Batteries recharged' (34). As he enjoys his newfound freedom, his cloths disappear one by one and he keeps gazing through a map of his motherland with mountains, ghats, deserts, sea and land. He struggles to locate his township from where he began his expedition.

His attention is drawn by a female voice from behind addressing him amorously as her Sindbad. She requests him to take her along on his journey like the great sailor Sindbad. As she is determined to go along with him, the cyclist cries for his Pa who appears and tells his that he is present only in his consciousness. His Pa advises him to shut his eyes to let everything disappear. 'Let her come. As I always say 'eyes closed, mountain gone.' If you don't see her, she doesn't exist' (36). Suddenly he realises that his clothes have all disappeared. In the meantime a Mermaid appears claiming to be princess Madalsa: 'I'm under a curse... the curse of an evil king. I am a princess. I can sing, dance, speak 53 languages. You have won my heart, Sindbad!'

(37). She wants to join him in his world tour like the way Sindbad went on his voyage on his magic carpet. She wants him to defeat the demon and set her free from the curse. As he searches for his clothes the mermaid tells him, 'If you got back your clothes, you'll run away from me, somewhere far... thinking that I swallowed your clothes... I will guard them for nine months in my womb... your clothes. Then I'll give birth to a lovely child. A child in your clothes...He will call you Pa, Pa. Papa, and me, Ma. Ma.'

He asks for his clothes threatening to call his Pa and Amma. But no Pa appears like in the past, instead the mermaid keeps dancing around.

13. The following sequence is that of the scene shifting to a man opening an imaginary door expressing his irritation being woken up from sleep. He is the same old Jogeshtey uncle who tells him to go to sleep.

    MAIN CHARACTER: Sleep? I am on my journey... journey of my world...
    on this bike.
    MAN: On this bicycle? There are no wheels on this bicycle, you stupid son of a
    Bitch. Did your father ever ride a bike without wheels? How can one travel on a cycle with no wheels? Idiot... Enough of your world tour and our sleepless nights!

14. As the man slams the imaginary door and disappears, the main character is left alone sulking in his loneliness. He mumbles planning to register his protest against Jogeshtey uncle to his Pa and Amma.

Speaking like a little kid, the main character wanders around the bicycle. Frightened and eyes closed he curls around the cycle and sleeps with his back to the audience. Spotlighting the bald patch on his head, the play ends with an enigmatic symbolism.

It is very puzzling for the reader/audience to understand why Tendulkar has written such an absurd play very different from all the others written over the decades. Probing into the various sequences I have listed, the play can be compared to Beckett's *Waiting for Godot* where 'Godot' could be identified with God, hope, love, death, a French cyclist (Prasad 88). 'Nothing' is central to both the plays.

Tendulkar writes like a true existentialist for whom man freely decides his future by the choices he makes and his actions. The play depicts absurd situations of life presented through the various sequences. Though the Main Character is told to do 'nothing' by his Pa, many things happen as the play progresses with a lot of action. The playwright delves into ' man's existential loneliness' (Deshpande 19). His protagonists have to stand all alone making their existential choice in life and bear the consequences of their decisions.

The play sums up the various strands of existential human predicament Tendulkar has examined through all his plays and attempts to communicate the view that, 'we may believe that everything is meaningless – nevertheless the quest for meaning remains an essential part of our apparently meaningless life' (Roubiczek 6).

The play does not have a beginning, a middle and an end as in a well structured play. It begins and ends irrationally. The play projects meaninglessness of human condition and leaves the readers/audience awestricken due to its unintelligible nature.

The play is deplete with exaggerated physical action that arouse comic laughter. It begins with the cyclist addressing the audience : 'The year? Which year is it? The year is? (*He remembers. Happily he takes a marker from his pocket and writes the current year on the banner. He puts the marker back in his pocket, then satisfied, rubs his hands.)* Finally, all set. Ready to roll (Tendulkar 6). Though the trip is well planned, he has his reservations regarding last minute hitches and says, '...And if you are starting out on a major trip, well – there's no end to things to take into account. One or two things wouldn't matter, but you must think about a thousand and one thing ' (6). At the end of the play it is evident that nothing has really happened with regard to his cycle tour from the beginning till the end as he is back on stage ready to undertake an expedition: '...Then I'll cut open the fish's stomach...take out my clothes to go on my travel... the world travel... the journey of the world on the bicycle...' (40). The lack of movement is representative of absurdity of human life. The final scene shows how the main character becomes younger and younger like a frightened child falling asleep beside the bicycle. The focus light on the bald patch on the back of his head is symbolic of the irony of life. Though he grows in age as time passes on, he has not achieved anything in life remaining still a child of his dream.

The playwright explores the basic predicament of modern man who lives a meaningless life. Like the cyclist he is fully involved in the action of going around the world, but his action does not make any progress. He stands still on his wheelless bicycle. This is the irony of life as man lives a purposeless life caught between life and death. At the end nothing remains except a dream as Ben Okri would opine 'A dream can be the highest point of life' (Okri, Ben 573).

The Cyclist is a superb absurd and black comedy presenting 'bizarre characters in bizarre situations' (Peck 86) creating a depressing atmosphere with jokes, farce and violence. As a black comedy it is crammed with cynical attitude to life based on the belief that man exists in a purposeless universe. It causes bitter laughter and amusement dealing with grim realities of life, giving an effect of insanity as well. The play is also a metaphor of self that is in a continuous process of life and death. For the playwright life is not definite as it revolves around unpredictable situations - begins and ends in void. Hence man is a helpless victim and there is 'nothing to be done' as Estragon utters in Beckett's *Waiting for Godot*. The predicament of life continues to perplex the cyclist who goes on his cyclic journey of life: 'the world travel… the journey of the world on the bicycle…' (Tendulkar 40).

References

Abjijeet. "In a conversation with Sir Vijay Tendulkar," December 19, 2006. (www passionforcinema.com/a-conversation-with-sir-vijay-tendulkar)

Bahadur, Sona. "The Legend Endures. 'The Indian Express. October 20, 1999.(Endureshttp://www.indianexpress.com/res/web/pIe/ie/daily/19991020/ile20071.html)

Deshpande, V.B. "Vijay Tendulkar's Contribution to Indian Drama."

Vijay Tendulkar's Plays: An Anthology of Recent Criticism. Ed. V.M. Madge. Delhi: Pencraft International, 2007.

Emmanuel, Steven M. "Kierkegaard, Soren Aabye." *Encyclopaedia of Philosophy*. 2nd Edition. Vol.5. Ed. Donald M. Borchert. USA: Macmillan Reference, 2006.

Friedman, Maurice.Ed. *The World of Existentialism: A Critical Reader*. New Jersey: Humanities Press International, 1991.

Kierkegaard, Soren. *Anxiety as the Presupposition of Hereditary Sin*. Trans. Reidar Thomte. New Jersey: Princeton University Press, 1980.

Okri, Ben. *The Famished Road*.London: Vintage, 2003.

Peck, John, and Martin Coyle. *Literary Terms and Criticism*. 2nd ed. London: Macmillan, 1993.

Prasad, G.J.V. Ed. *Waiting For Godot*. Delhi: Pearson Longman, 2006.

Roubiczek, Paul. *Existentialism For and Against*. London: Oxford University Press, 1964.

Sebastian, A.J, Chandra, N.D.R. *Literary Terms in Drama, Theatre and Cinema*. New Delhi: Authorspress, 2002.

Tendulkar, Vijay. *The Cyclist, His Fifth Woman*. New Delhi: Oxford University Press, 2006.

5

Miss Benare's Predicament in Vijay Tendulkar's *Silence! The Court is in Session*

Vijay Tendulkar's *Silence! The Court is in Session*, is an intense social criticism, satirizing the norms and traditions of society. It is a play with in a play in which a theatre group of teachers rehearse a play to be staged in a village. The rehearsal cannot progress as one of the cast, Prof. Damle, is absent. They ask one of the stagehands to fill in the gap. A mock court trial is staged to explain to the substitute cast the intricacies of the trial scene. The mock trial is staged on a charge of infanticide against one of the cast, Miss Benare. But the mock trial, instead, turns out to be the real story of Miss Benare who aborted Prof. Damle's illegitimate child, to protect their honour. The play-acting exposes the real crime of infanticide by Miss Benare which she finally acknowledges. The sequences, however, reveals the way she stands trial under a male dominated cast that silences her. A vociferous teacher like Miss Benare is unable to articulate herself before the malicious attacks of the witnesses. Hence, her silence remains a mystery until she speaks out the truth, calling for an iota of compassion. Tendulkar very deftly does not arrive at a final solution to the problem of infanticide, but questions the middle-class morality of complacency.

She breaks down as the troupe corners her into blocking all her chances of exit from the court room until she breaks down with her confession. The male harassment and high handed sadism by the rest of the cast turns the play meant to make villagers aware of social maladies, into a forced confession of her sin.

The title of the play *Silence! The Court is in Session* is a common expression by judges in law courts to bring order in the midst of disorder, establishing the absoluter power of the judge. The judge is the final authority to decide the case and decree his verdict.

In the play the dramatist depicts corruption that creeps into the legal system where even the judge becomes an oppressor lacking sense of natural justice and compassion. It also proves male domination in a patriarchal social system. The legal system is not effective enough to protect such victims from social menace. The cast is present surrounding Benaire like vultures in course of the play to eat into her vitals. Hér only mistake is getting impregnated by Prof. Damle, who remains off stage throughout the sequences.

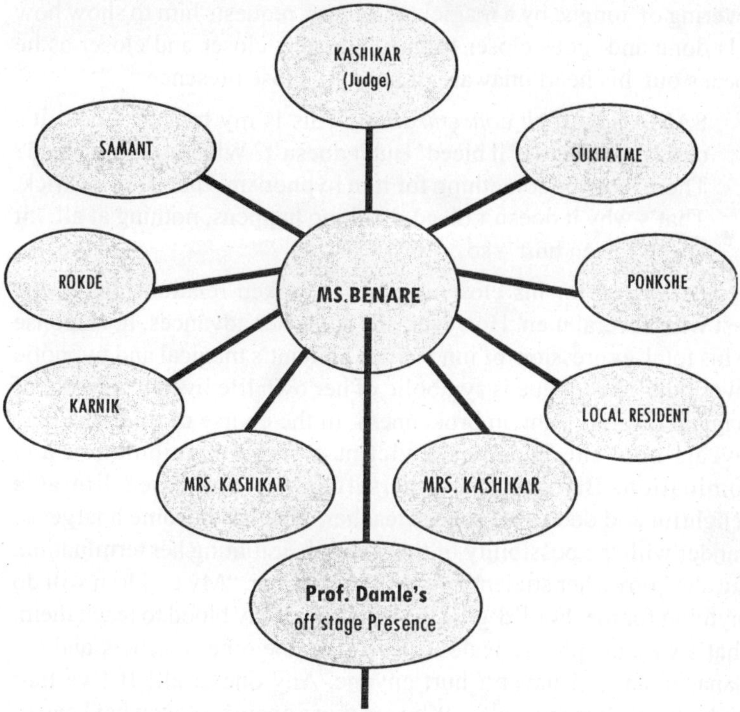

The play opens with the drama troupe on their way to the village hall where they are to rehearse the performance. Samant, a young man from the village, accompanies fast paced Miss Benare to the hall as the rest trail behind. Entering the hall he notices her sucking her finger and concludes she has hurt herself with the rusty bolt. He tells her to keep sucking the finger lest it swells later. She, on the contrary, reveals that she did it purely out of habit and expresses her happiness in being alone with him. She speaks of her desire to be free and go somewhere along with Samant in the absence of others.

> BENARE: Yes, I like you very much.
> SAMANT: Tut-tut. Ha ha! I'm hardly...
> BENARE: You're very nice indeed. And shall I tell you something?
> You are a very pure and good person. I like you (*STC* 56).

Samant further reveals that he is unmarried and witnesses all the shows put up at the village hall. He recounts how a magic show showed severing of tongue by a magician. Benare requests him to show how it is done and goes closer to him. She gets closer and closer as he speaks out his heart unaware of her very close presence.

> SAMANT: (*with concentration*) This is my tongue. Look, it's cut! Now what? It'll bleed! But it doesn't? Why doesn't it bleed? There must be something for it in hypnotism- that is, some trick. That's why it doesn't bleed. Nothing happens, nothing at all...it doesn't even hurt – so... (57).

She longed for his closeness in her broken relationships in the past with several men. However, she stops her advances, in response to his total expression of innocence. Samant's magical and hypnotic severing of the tongue is symbolic of her own life lived in a world of magical mystery sunk in brokenness. In the course of time, the play reveals how she becomes a victim of male manipulation and domination. Benare asserts herself in her oppressed life as a delightful and dedicated school teacher. She has become a target of slander with the possibility of the school initiating her termination. But she knows her students would stand by her. "My children will do anything for me. For I'd give the last drop of my blood to teach them. That's why people are jealous. Specially the other teachers and the management... I haven't hurt anyone. Any one at all! If I've hurt anybody, it's been myself...Who are these people to say what I can or can't do? My life is my own – I haven't sold it to anyone for a job! My will is my own. My wishes are my own...I'll do what I like with myself and my life! I'll decide..." (58). She affirms her identity as a person as has been pointed out, "One of the primal and seminal concerns of feminism is to declare that a woman is a being. She is not an appendage of man... She is an autonomous being, capable of, through trial and error, finding her own way to salvation" (Ramamoorthi 37). While speaking her heart out unconsciously she keeps her hand on her stomach, signifying her pain of having aborted her child. Samant is embarrassed to know of her pain and hurt feeling. She confesses how she feels so scared when alone. Suddenly she begins to clasp hands and sings out her heart, letting out her suppressed self and the emotional turmoil caused by falsely trusting men in her life.

> Oh, I've got a sweetheart
> Who carries all my books,
> He plays in my doll house,
> And says he likes my looks,
> I'll tell you a secret-
> He wants to marry me.
> But mummy says, I'm too little
> To have such thoughts as these (*STC* 58-9).

The song typifies her emotional life, seeking fulfilment in relationships with several men who finally betrayed her. She became a mere plaything in their hands for their sexual satisfaction with no emotional attachment leading to marriage. Her wounded femininity makes her a mere doll in the hands of men like the way the Nora utters in Ibsen's *A Doll's House:* "...You only thought how nice it was to be in love with me... At home, Daddy...used to call me his baby doll, and he played with me as I used to play with my dolls. Then I came to live in your house......I have been living here like a beggar...It's your fault that I've never made anything of my life...I have been your doll wife...I thought it was fun when you came and played with me" (Ibsen 82-3).

Benare articulates vibrantly as the play begins, interacting with her colleagues assertively, establishing her identity as an individual. "I, Leela Benare, a living woman, I say it from my own experience. Life is not meant for anyone else, It's your own life. It must be. It's a very, very important thing. Every moment, every bit of it is precious" (*STC* 61). In the course of the conversation, she tells that as a child she used to write on her well covered books. "The grass is green,/ The rose is red./ This book is mine/ Till I am dead" (62). But the truth of the matter is that all her books were torn into shreds, "torn one by one and went I don't know where – but I am still here. I am not dead! Not dead! The grass is still green, the rose is still red, but I am not dead" (62). So saying she keeps hysterically laughing, letting her subconscious of thwarted love life, which perhaps her colleagues knew to some extent. She goes on to recite a poem giving further revelation of the unconscious in her frustrated life:

> Our feet tread on upon unknown
> And dangerous pathways evermore.
> Wave after blinded wave is shattered
> Stormily upon the shore.
> Light glows alive again. Again
> It mingles with the dark of night.
> Our earthen hands burn out, and then
> Again in flames they are light,
> Everything is fully known,
> And everything is clear to see.
> And the wound that's born to bleed
> Bleeds on for ever, faithfully.
> There is a battle sometimes, where
> Defeat is destined as the end
> Some experiences are meant
> To taste, then just waste and spend (62-3).

Her life struggle is compressed in the poem, however, her colleagues take the cue to betray her spontaneity and expose her past and the complications of relationships with several men.

Since Prof. Damle fails to turn up for the rehearsal, they ask one of the stagehands to take his place. The rest of the play is built on the mock court scene in which Benare is tried, being accused of infanticide. Kashikar playing the role of a judge announces: "Prisoner Miss Benare, under section No. 302 of the Indian Penal Code, you have been accused of the crime of infanticide. Are you guilty or not guilty of the aforementioned crime?" (75). The serious atmosphere of the court scene is interspersed with comical episodes of pan eating and passing on beedis, to show it as only a game-play. But Miss Benare gets tensed up though she pretends to be light hearted. Her reactions are very thought out. As the interrogation progresses Kashikar states that he picked up such a case for study to show the serious social implications of such crimes. Al! the characters agree with him on the seriousness of the crime, isolating Benare who wants to change the topic of debate. "Why don't you accuse me instead of - um – snatching public property!" (78). Unrelenting, Kashikar reprimands her for obstructing the procedure of the court in session. She tries to reasons with him and pleads not guilty. As she couldn't even think of killing a common cockroach, how could she ever kill a newborn child? Instead of sympathy from the others, she gets a battery of good thoughts from Sukhatme who refers to the nobility of motherhood and to consider worshipping women as mother of mankind. In accordance with social customs, she is told it is her bounden duty to protect and preserve her little ones.

The judge makes the witnesses take oath on Oxford English Dictionary, adding to the comical nature of the mock trial. But when it comes to the question of the trial of Benare, they are damned serious with their malicious determination to have it out with her past affairs and her unmarried status. One by one, the vultures, enter the witness box to give false witness. Benare, though tensed up, pretends to laugh away unrestrainedly. Rokde begins to recount how he had seen Benare in the house of Prof. Damle at dusk. Though she protests at introducing something irrelevant to the mock trial, they continue harassing her. They even make Samant give witness against her in a mock manner as though he had seen her at Prof. Damle's house in the night. He gives a cooked up account of having heard the crying of a woman in the house. Benare gets upset with the mock trial going in the wrong direction and goes into a rage demanding that it be stopped. She decides to leave, suspecting them to have plotted against her. But she could only boil with rage: "Note it down. Note everything down! Just take down note after note!" (94). Her eyes full of tears, she is defiant. She picks up her bag to leave, but the door is bolted and locked.

Act III continues with the trial. But Benare stands silent and still. She is dragged into the witness box .She begins to reveal her terror like a trapped animal. She remains silent deliberately as they keep accusing her of her crime. Kashikar is determined to take steps to deal with the prisoner's refusal to answer. She is given ten seconds to respond. As she continues to maintain silence, the judge digs up the question of marrying girls before puberty so that they cannot continue to flirt with men. She is questioned as to why she remained a spinster even in such an advanced age. As she continues to maintain silence, they taunt her with several filthy queries. Mrs. Kashikar opines that Benare kept off marriage with selfish motive of trying to get everything without marrying. Benare used to be dropped home after every performance by Prof. Damle. She refers to "everything" meaning freedom and promiscuity in her relationship with Prof. Damle and other men.

Rokde takes stock of the situation and plucks up courage to accuse Benare of having made advances to him once, after a performance.

> ROKDE: She held my – my hand...I said- 'This isn't proper... I don't like this at all...
> I freed my hand. She moved away. She said, 'Don't tell anyone what happened.'
> BENARE: That's a lie!

She breaks her silence to retort, but no one pays any heed. On the other hand, they encouraged Rokde to continue his maligning her character.

Next in line, it is Ponkshe who takes up the character assassination of the distressed girl. He gives proof of Benare keeping a bottle of TIK-20 in her purse. Once, he was given a sealed envelope through one of her school children, asking him to meet her urgently at Udipi restaurant. He further added that she made known her desire to marry him since she was impregnated by Prof. Damle. She made him promise never to disclose it to any one. After that it happened that a bottle of TIK-20 rolled out of her purse. When he refused her plea, she got worked up and threatened Ponkshe. Karnik also informs the court that she had attempted suicide due to disappointment in love. She had fallen in love when fifteen years with her own maternal uncle. Kashikar also refers to the plan of the management of the school to dismiss such an immoral woman from service. As she hears all these accusations, Benare takes a small bottle of TIK-20 to put into her mouth, but Karnik dashes forward to strikes it away. As the story unfolds, the judge orders Prof. Damle to appear in court to witness. But his failure to turn up makes the situation more grievous for Benare, unable to get justice.

Sukhatme, acting as counsel for the prosecution, condemns her immoral life and begs the court to deliver fitting punishment as "the accused is public enemy number one. If such socially destructive tendencies are encouraged to flourish, this country and its culture will be totally destroyed" (114). He continues to argue how motherhood without marriage is unethical and a great sin. He accuses her of having plotted to dynamite the very roots of religion. It is very evident that "the institution of motherhood is controlled by man and this physical quality conditions her entire life" (Rich 35). Such patriarchal male domination does not allow Benare any space for getting fair justice.

Before the sentence is passed the judge asks if she has any thing to say in defence. A motionless Benare stands up erect and begins to speaks out, breaking her silence after a long time. She refers to her life like a book being ripped into pieces. "Life is a poisonous snake that bites itself. Life is a betrayal. Life is a fraud. Life is a drug. Life is a drudgery. Life is a something that's nothing – or a nothing that's something" (116). She reveals how she lost all belief in emotions and sentiments. She had fallen in love with her maternal uncle when a teenager. She had not known what sin was then. She couldn't fulfil her dream as her brave uncle took to his heels. Betrayed and bitter, she threw herself off the parapet to die. But failed in her attempt. Again she fell in love as a grown up woman. "I offered up my body on the altar of my worship. And my intellectual god took the offering – and went his way. He didn't want my mind, or my devotion…He was a man. For whom everything was of the body, for the body…This body is a traitor" (117-8). Writhing in pain she expresses her disgust for her body, yet she loves it. She had only one desire to live for her child. "I want my body now for him – for him alone…He must have a mother… a father to call his own – a house – to be looked after – he must have a good name!" (118). Rejecting her plea to marry her, Prof. Damle wanted to protect his honour, disregarding her honour, in the midst of a mutual sexual pervasion. The condemnation meted out to her by the court is based on the social norm that "Marriage is the destiny traditionally offered to women by society. It is still true that most women are married, or have been, or plan to be, or suffer from not being (Beauvoir 445). Hence in the play Benare is ignored as an individual and condemned for her sin with a man who does not invite any condemnation. His colleagues refer to Prof. Damle as a "calculating" (*STC* 68) man who used to sit comfortably at home whenever there is some hindrance to his programmes. This is also shown in his sexually perverse life, when he refused to make restitution for his crime of impregnating Benare.

The court decrees that there is no forgiveness for her crime since marriage is the very foundation of social stability with motherhood being sacred and pure. The verdict is passed that she should live while her child in her womb should be destroyed. Benare writhes in pain and refuses to abide by the judgement and collapses.

The sequence shifts to the curious faces gathered to witness the dramatic performance. Sukhatme rounds up everything saying that they had some good fun just like fighting a real case, though it was only a game-play. As all withdraw to get ready for the show, Samant calls her out. But getting no response, he places the green cloth parrot which he had bought for his niece, near her. The play ends with Benare's own voice singing softly from somewhere the song of the parrot:

> The parrot to the sparrow said,
> 'Why, oh why, are your eyes so red?
> 'Oh, my dear friend, what shall I say?
> Someone has stolen my nest away' (121).

Tendulkar examines how women are often "silenced and suppressed in a male dominated social order" (Oslen 37), which is portrayed in the case of Benare who finds no sympathy from her accusers. She becomes a victim of "gendered subaltern" (Spivak 267), when even a woman like Mrs. Kashikar doesn't show any compassion. She goes silent due to "female bonding" (Furman 182) as she is unable to articulate herself, being unnerved by the evil machination of the men surrounding her.

It has been a very absorbing discussion play like those of Ibsen or Bernard Shaw. The presentation of a play-within-a-play, highlighting social issues, becomes a calculated attack on the central character through a mock trial. The evil of oppression of women in the name of sacred social traditions, continue to haunt through the character assassination of Benare.

The play is also a scathing satirical attack on legal profession where a right can be made wrong and vice versa. The sacredness of the court in session is marred by comical taking of oath on the Oxford English Dictionary and pan eating with time allotted for spitting.

Silence! The Court is in Session is a superb social criticism of male domination in society by which "..women have often been called upon to make sacrifices, adjust and accommodate claims of religion and moralities and suppress their personal claims...Women have often been left waiting on the margin" (Jain 9). Through the play, Tendulkar makes a clarion calls for introspection on gender inequality and inhuman social norms and conventions forced upon the weaker sex.

Works Cited

Beauvoir, Simone De. *The Second Sex*. Trans. H.M. Parshley. London: Vintage, 1997.

Furman, Nelly. "The Study of Women and Language." *Comment*, Vol. 3, No.3, Autumn, 1978.

Ibsen, *A Doll's House*. New Delhi: Oxford University Press, reprt. 2004.

Jain, Jasbir & A.K. Singh.Eds. *Indian Feminisms*. New Delhi: Creative Books, 2001.

Oslen, Tillie. *Silences*. New York: Delacorte, 1978.

Ramamoorthi, P. "My Life is My Own: A Study of Sashi Deshpande's Women." *Indian Women Novelists.* Vol. V. Ed. R.K. Dhawan. New Delhi:Prestige, 1995.

Rich, Adrienne. *Of Women Born: Motherhood as Experience and Institution*. New York: W.W. Norton, 1976.

Spivak, Gayatri Chakravorty. "A Literary Representation of Subaltern: A Woman's Text from the Third World." *In Other Worlds: Essays in Cultural Politics*. London: Routledge, 1988.

Tendulkar, Vijay. "Silence! The Court is in Session." *Five Plays.* New Delhi: Oxford University Press, reprt 2007, 53-121. Abbreviated *STC.*

6

Human Predicament in the Selected Plays of Asif Currimbhoy

I do not subscribe to the opinion that Indian Drama is yet to establish itself as a viable genre (Naik, Shyamala 2007:201). Though unacknowledged in comparison to poetry and fiction, Indian drama is there to stay with the dramatic output of playwrights such as Sri Aurobindo, T.P. Kailasam, Tagore, Harindranath Chattopadhyaya, G.V. Desani, Lakhan Deb, A.S.P. Ayyar, Lobo-Prabhu, Fyzee Rahamin, Asif Currimbhoy, Nissim Ezekiel, Gieve Patel, Partap Sharma, Mohan Rakesh, Badal Sircar, Vijay Tendulkar, Girish Karnad, Shiv K. Kumar, Mahasweta Devi, Gurcharan Das, M.V. Rama Sarma, Manohar Malgonkar, J.P. Das, Mahesh Dattani, Dina Mehta, Manjula Padmanabhan, Uma Parameswaran, T.S. Gill and Shashi Tharoor. Often drama is used as a synonym for play; however, there is a slight difference between the two. A play is a drama meant to be performed before a theatrical audience (Murfin 97).

Though several plays have been written in India dealing with a variety of social issues, there are very few who have written plays which can be stage produced. This is where Currimbhoy (1928-1975) has his singular position by producing realistic plays for the stage. In all he had produced 29 plays in 17 years of intense creative output despite his work as a senior Company Executive of the Burmah Shell Oil Company. Born a Khoja Muslim, he had his early education in a Jesuit School. Graduating in Economics from Berkeley University in California, he had a wide range of experiences abroad. His study of the Indian classics like the *Ramayana*, the *Mahabharata*, the *Gita* and the Upanishads coupled with the western exposure he had, brought about a synthesis of the Eastern and the Western cultures in his writings (Agrawal 1-2).

He is considered the first dramatist to show great interest in producing plays by fusing elements of pantomime, dance and song (Reddy 216). He is also believed to be the most prolific among the Indian dramatists contriving interesting situations with a great sense of atmosphere (Iyengar 245). He wrote his plays based on what he observed in life. 'There is a sense of trigger – I think the trigger was life itself, of what I saw around, of how I reacted to it, in other words an emotional reaction' (Currimbhoy, February 1976 :39).

Currimbhoy explores universal human predicament through his social, moral, religious and political concerns in the plays. He is a voice of universal revolt and anguish. And it is compassion that unifies his plays (Currimbhoy 1993a:ix). Sensing conflicts everywhere he says,'...conflict in theatre, conflict at every level – physical, mental, emotional – because from the time really you meet with other people, what is called human relationships' (Rajinder, Jacob. December1970). This paper is an attempt to give a bird's eye-view of the human situation and predicament handled by the playwright in his selected plays.

He has been very prolific as a playwright dealing with social, political, religious and psychological issues in plays such as *The Tourist Mecca* (1959), *The Clock* (1959), *The Doldrummers* (1960), *The Dumb Dancer* (1961), *OM* (1961), *Thorns on a Canvas* (1962), *The Captives* (1963), *Goa* (1964), *The Hungry Ones* (1965), *Valley of the Assassins* (1966), *The Temple Dancers* (1967), *The Lotus Eater* (1967), *Abbe Faria* (1968), *The Mercenary* (1968), *An Experiment with Truth* (1969), *The Great Indian Bustard* (1970), *Inquilab* (1970), *Darjeeling Tea?* (1971), *The Refugee* (1971), *Sona Bangla* (1972), *Om Mane Padme Hum!* (1972), *The Miracle Seed* (1973), *Angkor* (1973), *The Dissident MLA* (1974), and *This Alien... Native Land* (1975).

Inquilab, *The Refugee* and *Sonar Bangla,* clubbed together as Bengal trilogy, are set in the background of the Naxalite revolt that haunted West Bengal; the refugee problem faced by the state in the wake of unrest in the freedom struggle for Bangladesh; and the Indo-Pak war. In these plays, K.R. Srinivasa Iyengar finds that the playwright has scrutinised the basic human condition and portrayed the agonised expression of his social conscience (Currimbhoy 1993a:iii). In *Inquilab* Currimbhoy affirms that the Naxal shortcut is no happy solution to any problem and that evil and hatred can be overcome only through love and understanding. In *The Refugee* he portrays refugees of all times in the struggle of Yassin. *Sona Bangla* is symbolic representation of the eternal struggle of humanity against suppression and oppression (Reddy 52).

Inquilab while depicting the Naxalite struggle in Bengal, probes into the way violence breaks loose. The play focuses on Prof. Datta who finds his students resorting to violence propounded by the Marxists. Datta finds it impossible to continue persuading his students with his Gandhian ideals. His son Amar tries to convince him of the Marxist ideologies when he affirms – 'This is my passion, my poetry, my cause. Look around father, open your eyes: the poverty, the terrible poverty. People dying of hunger, father. Look at the gap between rich and poor. It's growing, father, dangerously… and unfairly. It's true, the city is dying, your old beloved city of the privileged' (Currimbhoy 1993a:13). The revolution takes its toll. Datta is killed by his own elder son who is a Naxal extremist. Jain the landlord is another victim of violence. Finally Amar comes to the realization that his father was right in upholding the Gandhian principles: '…my father was right…that change should come through the will of the majority…expressed through a free vote…I've found my path…and it will be the same as that of my father' (80-1). The play ends symbolically with Ahmed confirming his stand of pursuing his Marxist revolution, while Prof. Datta's wife observing Ahmed, picks up healthy rice seeds from a tray and flings into fertile soil. The play pictures the futility of Marxist ideology bringing destruction through revolution.

The Refugee is a drama of social realism portraying the misery of the Bangladesh refugees in the 1970s. The story revolves around Yassin, a refugee from East Pakistan who gets involved in the liberation of his land joining Mukti Bahini. Coming to Bengal as a refugee Yassin is given shelter by Sengupta who was himself a refugee. Inspired by Sengupta's children Mita and Ashok, Yassin takes up the challenge to liberate his people. Mita tells him:

> Oh Yassin, touch me! Can't you see I'm a human being? Can't you see I'm real? Aren't you moved? The refugees exist the same way. They're alive…only too real. They bring tears to my eyes, their suffering touches my heart. I can't bear to leave them alone.

> All of life draws me…the human condition…if all of us were to…abstain the way you do, we'd be doing harm…done through neglect (Currimbhoy 1993b:29).

Yassin can not continue anymore to live in his comfort zone as he is emotionally determined to join the freedom struggle. 'I almost said "nothing" through force of habit. But something has. The inevitable. Man really has little choice in life. He is often forced into a situation…where there is no way out. A decision, an action…gets destined, almost involuntarily' (40).

The play is a superb analysis of the human predicament that the central characters face in the wake of the refugee crisis in Bengal. More than the refugee-rehabilitation programme, the play portrays the ideological conflict in the various characters who are caught up between the forces of nationalism and humanism. Finally Yasssin plunges into action setting aside his non-committal attitude (577). Srinivasa Iyengar rendered the characters and actions of the play universal when he opined that the "Refugee" is Yassin – he is also Sengupta – he is any refugee, he is all refugees (Currimbhoy 1993a:vi). Reflecting on the refugee problem Currimbhoy himself stated, 'A mistake committed at a particular point of time seem to have a cumulative effect, and one inevitably gets drawn into it all' (Currimbhoy 2006d:71).

Sonar Bangla is built around both external and internal conflicts. External conflicts consist of those between : East & West Pakistan; Hindus and Muslims in East Pakistan; Bengali Muslims and guerillas. All these in the backdrop of the refugee crisis leads to Indo-Pak war and the emergence of Bangladesh. The internal conflict is shown through characters like Hussain and Mujib. When the war breaks out Hussain articulates his fears, 'But I was just thinking… of the pain and scars that're going to tear my Bangla once again.' (Currimbhoy 1993c: 87). Mujib when he returns to Bangladesh after his release from solitary confinement gives vent to his internal conflict in the final soliloquy, '…I never wept during all those months in solitary confinement. I never wept when they put me on trial. But I wept when I arrived back here and saw my wonderful Sonar Bangla' (104). Currimbhoy himself was agonized by the war and wrote, 'The war is a tragedy. Can't understand why others don't see it the same way. The blood flows – the hysteria grips all opponents' (Bowers 1993d:71).

An Experiment with Truth while exploring the works and martyrdom of Gandhiji, is an intense psychological study of human frailty. Through stream of consciousness the play presents bare facts of life 'that great men have great faults; also a great sense of achievement' (Currimbhoy 1976:47). Through the various episodes the playwright probes into the major events in the life of the Mahatma culminating in his assassination. The episodes take us through Gandhiji's fast unto death to bring unity among Hindus and Muslims, Salt march, conflict with Kasturba etc. The play hinges on external and internal conflicts. The play opens with Gandhi summing up his central motif in a feeble voice:

> What is the hunger of the stomach compared to the bleeding of the heart? I fast as much for myself, my own penitence, as I do for you, your own salvation…That millions should die, slain by our own hands…when our quest in life was one of peace and non-violence…When I strove for freedom of our nation, I also strove for freedom of our soul. There can be no freedom without brotherhood between Hindus and Muslims, without unity with Sikhs and Christians (Currimbhoy 1993d:10).

The playwright salutes Gandhiji as a beacon of light to bring hope in a broken world as Sheean utters, '…If the hand of God did not save him from assassin's bullet, was it because He wanted to take him away?...through darkness and fear, courage and light in this our mortal plight…never will I forget…this man who led me, his kindly light…' (66).

Goa is a realistic play based on the story of an Indian boy's love for a Goan girl. The story is woven around multiple relationships. Rose is central to the story as she is woed by both Krishna and Alphonso. Alphonso describes her, 'Rose is Goa and Goa is Rose' (Currimbhoy 1993e:41) and frequently visits them with presents. Her mother Miranda wants both the men to court her instead. The story climaxes in Krishna murdering Alphonso and later raping Rose. The play ends as Krishna's 'nude body falls out, with a dagger in his heart' (Ibid.92). The story is symbolic of Goa's freedom struggle. Portuguese made Goa an enclave over four hundred years ago. Goa still continued under slavery for 14 years after Indian independence in 1947. The playwright employs the socio-realistic plotting and the play is made an allegory where rape and personal abuse lead to suffering and disintegration (Meserve 12).

Om Mane Padme Hum brings out powerfully the Chinese experienced. The title is derived from the Buddhist chant "Om Mane Padme Hum" (Hail to the Jewel in the Lotus) being recited by the monks along with young Rimpoche in the Lhasa monastery. The General Chang Chin-wn leading the military to occupy Tibet does not cause bloodshed harming Dalai Lama; instead he instructs his forces to usher in a new cultural revolution: 'This is a grand mission. We're not here merely to liberate or occupy but to stay, stay and fortify. Stay and integrate. From this roof of the world...' (Currimbhoy 1992a: 37). The new cultural revolution is aimed at replacing Buddhism with Communism. As the National oppression surges, conflicts continue to daunt Dalai Lama and the other characters. When the three Abbots ask him to leave Tibet for his personal safety, Dalai Lama refuses saying, '...Why should I leave? They'll kill me? So I shall leave this body. There'll be a 14th ... and 15th Dalai Lama (13). The mother of Dalai Lama does not want to renounce him as her child as he is deified and in danger of being killed by the Chinese. As Srinivasa Iyengar observes the play involves something more than the Lama's or Tibet's fortunes and it is masterly in juxtaposing of opposites such as Lamaism and Communism; Beauty and the Beast; the Past and the Future; Violence and Sufferance (Iyengar 93). As the Tibetan struggle still continues, the playwright makes the audience/readers experience the tension of the protagonist to a great extent. The play is more than a pictorial representation of living history as it is a universal comment on life (Bowers 6). In the wake of the recent Tibetan uprising, Dalai Lama said: 'I felt the same tension I felt 50 years ago... I cried for Tibet recently' (Roy, 1 April 2008).

The Hungry Ones takes us to the streets of Calcutta with its poverty, misery, riots and arson. The play is based on the visit of American beatnik-poet Allen Ginsberg and Peter Orlovsky to Calcutta many years ago. They moved around the streets of Calcutta in dirty khaki shorts and dishevelled beards (Currimbhoy 1992b: 21). The playwright brings out two Americans whose actions lead through the various strands in the play through satire, ridicule and humour. They try to involve themselves in various activities such as yoga, carpet-prayer etc. They try to understand the mystery of India with its hunger and poverty. Symbolically they can hear the voice of the woman representing the voices of Indians: 'So you want to become / one of us, stranger / a hungry one...? / then learn: stranger, learn.../ HUNGER! (30).

In the play symbols dominate with its cyclic movement. The Americans in their search seem to learn something, but what they learn is that they can never learn. The human predicament is well depicted in the final scene where the first scene recurs. Through the frustration of the Americans the playwright represents various insolvable conflicts existing in the Indian society making it still hungry and suffering (Meserve 18).

The story of *The Miracle Seed* is based on the drought that Maharashtra faced in 1972. The play takes us to the family of Ram that decides to leave for the city after two monsoon failures. Ram's nephew Laxman comes from the city with the miracle seed, promising a golden harvest, with the new agrarian revolution. Ram acknowledges him: 'He's full of ideas, you know...But over and over again he comes back to talking about the hybrid seed... Scientific farming, he calls it...We've ploughed and ploughed. Planted the seed. This entire season. He promises we'll reap...a golden harvest' (Currimbhoy 1973:20-21).

But the seeds do not germinate and the family is about to migrate to the city when the miracle takes place when Ram's daughter Savitri brings some hybrid stalks from her vegetable patch. At the same time Savitri is able to talk without stammering after the exercises with pellet stones in her mouth. Thus the play symbolically represents the green revolution as well as Savitri's restoration of speech.

Based on the political events that took place in Gujarat in 1974, *The Dissident M.L.A.* centres on the evil designs of Manu to topple the Government. The play depicts various incidents such as students' protest against raise in mess bill at the Engineering college hostel, tough examinations, corrupt Government etc. The agitating students gherao the Vice Chancellor and publicly humiliate the Home Minister, shaving his head, blackening his face and parading him riding on a donkey. The events finally lead to dissolution of the Gujarat Assembly. The play is a social criticism in which the playwright satirises politicians who are corrupt and greedy. Manu the M.L.A. uses his son Ramesh to mobilise student revolt to make political gains out of it. At the end of it all, corruption continues in spite of change of guard in administration as the father and son discuss:

> MANU: Where was the mistake? We… you and I… rooted out corruption.
>
> RAMESH: Did we? You know what that wise old fox told me? He said there'd be a new election, and new corrupt M.L.A.'s would come in instead of the old corrupt ones… It means we've gone through all this for nothing. We'll have the same old corrupt Government as long as people live (Currimbhoy1974:55).

OM and *The Dumb Dancer* are religious plays in which Currimbhoy makes his comment on religious yearning of people. *Om* presents man's search for God as he himself claimed, 'There is the mystical element in the human being that always drew me to the spiritual factor in life. I was not attracted to any particular religion; I was attracted to all. As a result I wrote separate plays on religion which are highly academic' (Currimbhoy 1976:48). In the play he attempts to present the basic philosophical concepts of Hinduism and the ways to salvation and moksa, basing himself on the Vedic and Upanishadic concepts. The Guru – Disciple discourse leads to the mystery of God. The Guru says, 'As the birds fly in the air, as the fish swim in the sea, leaving no traces behind, even so the pathway to God is traversed by the seeker of spirit' (Currimbhoy 1993f:73).

The Dumb Dancer takes us through the story of a *Kathakali* dancer, Bhima, who undergoes psychological and mental confusion, leading to insanity. He plays the role of Bhima in the dance play and believes that he has killed Duryodhana and has eaten his guts. Having been admitted into the mental asylum he is under the treatment of Dr. Prema. She arranges to give a shock therapy by showing him real human entrails. She also begins to communicate with the dumb dancer and allows him to caress her. While trying her psychiatric experiment on the dumb dancer, Dr. Prema herself falls into his arms and decides to kill Shakuntala. Dr. Prema is mesmerised by the dumb dancer and lets out her mind to Dr. Dilip:

> Who is sane, Dilip, and who is not? Remember, I tried, Dilip. Really tried. But it drew me closer instead of further. The vertigo… the vortex… I found myself slipping into the terrifying abyss of darkness…slipping, slipping without being able to hold

> myself back. How much of the insane fantasy was true and how much was not. Sanity lay...as a fine dividing line. It seemed to move...and engulf me. No words can tell you what its discovery means because it lies beyond... the point of no return. No greater passion was there than this stalwart God....When I touched him, I felt the element of distraction grow within me...The desperation grew. Identification. I searched for it. But the other image of myself lay in his world...not mine (Currimbhoy 1993g:80-81).

The play is an intense psychological study of man's frailty and emotions that become uncontrollable.

The Doldrummers brings before us people living meaningless lives such as the alienated Anglo-Indian youth Tony, Rita, Joe and Liza. They live very immoral and wayward lives. Rita is in love with Tony and longs for him. Tony is told of Rita's affair with the Fat and Bald Man, but he has no courage to encounter him. Liza becomes a professional prostitute in order to keep Tony to herself. It is Joe who happens to be the first to visit her. She carries Joe's child and refuses to abort it. However her love for Tony continues and when he returns with Moron Moe, she has no choice but to rush into the sea to end her life. Tony rushes after her and providentially both are saved. Meanwhile Joe commits suicide. The play ends with Tony singing a song about doldrums:

> Let's go my friend,
> We'll go together, my friend,
> To where the doldrums end.
> Never fear, old man,
> That's where it all began.
> Blind though we be,
> There's nothing left to see (Currimbhoy 1992c : 92).

The Tourist Mecca is written in the backdrop of tourists visiting Agra bringing to focus the story of two lovers, an American citizen, Janet, and Keshav, a local tourist guide. Janet is warned by her mother Lady Toppin that Keshav is a gigolo, a professional lover. Though Keshav vows his genuine love for her, she leaves promising to return the following year. The play ends Keshav whispering to himself, 'Goodbye, Janet, until next year... and the year after that... until love will have lost its meaning; but for no reason we'll still be there' (Currimbhoy 1993h:72). Though Keshav is a professional lover hired by foreign tourists, his genuine love for Janet remains a deep-rooted reality. The conflict in him between professional love and real love brings him to the brink of psychological breakdown.

Darjeeling Tea? is centred on the study of Big Mac a Darjeeling planter, his wife Jennie and his illegitimate daughter Didi from a local Nepali girl. Bunty, a young Indian planter falls in love with Didi adding romantic zest to the play. The play dramatises a serious conflict between levels of society. (Meserve, Walter 1992:11). Jennie had been living a conflicting and unhappy life for the past 19 years due to her husband's illicit relationship with a local woman. Jennie plans to leave India and says, 'I'm not leaving you, Mac. I'm just going away to Scotland. Like Hugh said, my offer's open… anytime. I'll be waiting there, Mac, I'll be waiting there… for you… No, don't say a word, Mac. Just look after yourself…You're the most precious thing I have… and I'll never forget you… Goodbye, love…' (Currimbhoy 1992d :51-53).

This Alien...Native Land is built around the life of an Indian middle-class Jewish family – Joseph and Rachel and their three children Jacob, David and Sarah. The family is in great predicament with their growing problems of joblessness and marital problems. Sarah unable to find a Jew to marry her, plans to settle with a married Muslim. But in the end she goes off to Israel. Jacob marries Tara, a divorcee who does not follow traditional religious practices of the family. The story further delves into problems such as - Rachel's oedipal relations with her sons; David's illicit affair with his brother's wife, etc. As the title suggests, they remain aliens in India, dreaming of the promised land. The psychological impact due to conflicts faced by the characters reveal many things related to the predicaments of that community. Their frustration is expressed by David when he speaks to his mother after the death of his father:

> A requiem. A requiem for the dead…in this, our native land… I'm sure he dreamed of flowers and a graveyard for the family, where his ghost could point proudly…to a family heritage. Lines of mourners, in greys and blacks, the fine drizzle of rain, with heads bent low…It wasn't quite like that, was it, Ma? The city swamped us, our brothers left, the graveyard decayed beyond

> death, the lilies festered, and there was the vulgar laugh of the not-so-dead…Oh father of mine, that I could have reburied you, in my arms… (Currimbhoy 1992e: 41-42).

Currimbhoy's plays are all centred on human predicament which puzzles him so much that he shares the pain and agony of humanity through the characters he creates. The pathetic human condition is uppermost in his mind. Hence, while expressing his compassion for mankind in doldrums, he draws the attention of his audience/ readers to become sympathizers in turn. His imagination is built on the experience of life. There is a perfect fusion of thought and feeling as 'the world of the mind as well as the social and political world that surround him… He has something to say… a message to deliver, a vision to fulfill and he must work, speak, write and act.' (Meserve10).

All his plays deal with serious social, political, moral and religious issues with pathos, sentiment, irony and social criticism. He also adds gentle comic laughter with a cynical and ironic purpose. Currimbhoy is considered India's first authentic voice in theatre writing plays of dissent (Bowers 1993d : viii). All his issues, though local in colour, are of universal appeal, drawing attention to problems of man everywhere such as denial of human rights, justice and freedom. This is evident from the appreciation he has received from theatres across the world, where the plays have been successfully staged. The conflicts presented are internal as well as external in nature, rendering them superb psychological studies. Scholars like M.K. Naik have pointed out certain incongruities in his work and art:

> Most of these plays have a strong 'documentary' element about them and there is no attempt to understand and project in dramatic terms the ideological implications of the political conflicts dealt within. The dramatist appears to be primarily interested in the thrill of the exciting events rather than the thought processes which shaped them. The result is sheer reportage; and when Currimbhoy gives free rein to his imagination, the upshot is often crude and contrived symbolism… Unless Currimbhoy realizes that drama is something more than simply play of lights, plethora of sounds and parade of violence, all his enviable

industry and enthusiasm are unlikely to produce viable and worthwhile plays (Naik, M.K 258-61).

Despite the flaws pointed out, his plays have been highly appreciated and successfully staged in several countries. A perceptive critic will also find it extremely difficult to separate his didacticism from his dramatic art. His dramatic techniques are meant 'to provide visual images to stimulate the minds, the ears, and the eyes of his audience' (Meserve 15). In the process he makes excellent use of monologues, choruses, pantomime, music and visual effects.

Currimbhoy's compassion for humanity is the central motif as he details out the predicament of man in agony and ecstasy. The plays are excellent studies in human behaviour. His purpose is to make his audience/readers appreciate life in its totality. In the process he presents social evils and chaos letting his audience/readers to find the right answers themselves. At the same time one gets the impression that the playwright is personally involved in the plays and uses the stage to present societal issues with the intention of social transformation. However the playwright does not like to be labelled a propagandist as he claims to let his audience make their conclusions from his presentation of facts (Currimbhoy, February 1976 :41).

Works Cited

Agrawal, K.A. *The Best Plays of Asif Currimbhoy*. Jaipur: Book Enclave, 2007.

Bowers, Faubion. "Afterword." *An Experiment with Truth*. 2nd ed. Calcutta: Writers Workshop, 1993d.

——. "Introduction.' *Om Mane Padme Hum*. 2nd ed. Calcutta: Writers Workshop, 1992a.

Currimbhoy, Asif. 1973. *The Miracle Seed*. Calcutta: Writers Workshop.

——. *The Dissident M.L.A.* Calcutta: Writers Workshop, 1974.

——. "Commentary Meets Asif Currimbhoy."*Commentary.* Vol. I. No..3. February, 1976.

——. *Om Mane Padme Hum.* 2nd ed. Calcutta: Writers Workshop,1992a.

——.*The Hungry Ones.* 3rd ed. Calcutta: Writers Workshop, 1992b.

——. *The Doldrummers.* Calcutta: Writers Workshop,1992c.

——. *Darjeeling Tea?* 2nd ed. Calcutta: Writers Workshop, 1992d.

——. *The Alien...Native Land.* 2nd ed. Calcutta: Writers Workshop, 1992e.

——. *Inquilab.* 2nd ed. Calcutta: Writers Workshop, 1993a.

——. *The Refugee.* 2nd ed. Calcutta: Writers Workshop, 1993b.

——. *Sonar Bangla.* 2nd ed. Calcutta: Writers Workshop,1993c.

——. *An Experiment with Truth.* 2nd ed. Calcutta: Writers Workshop, 1993d.

——. *Goa.* 3rd ed. Calcutta: Writers Workshop, 1993e.

——. *OM.* 2nd ed. Calcutta: Writers Workshop, 1993f.

——. *The Dumb Dancer.* 2nd ed. Calcutta: Writers Workshop, 1993g.

——. *The Tourist Mecca.* 2nd ed. Calcutta: Writers Workshop, 1993h.

Iyengar, K.R. Srinivasa. "Om Mane Padme Hum." *The Doldrummers.* Calcutta: Writers Workshop, 1992.

——.*Indian Writing in English.* 5th edition (reprint). New Delhi:Sterling Publishers Private Limited, 2002.

Meserve, Ruth & Walter Meserve. "Foreword." *The Hungry Ones.* Calcutta: Writers Workshop, 1992.

Murfin, Ross & Supryia Ray. *The Bedford Glossary of Critical and Literary Terms.* Bedford: Bedford Books, 1998.

Naik, M.K. *A History of Indian English Literature.* New Delhi: Sahitya Akademi, 1982.

Naik, M.K. & Shyamala A. Narayan. *Indian English Literature 1980-2000 : A Critical Survey.* Delhi: Pencraft International, 2007.

Rajinder, Paul & Jacob Paul. *Enact.* Interview with Currimbhoy. December, 1970.

Reddy, P. Bayapa. *The Plays of Asif Currimbhoy.* Calcutta. Writers Workshop, 1985.

Reddy, K. Venkata & Dhawan, R.K. *Flowering of Indian Drama: Growth and Development*. New Delhi: Prestige Books, 2004.

Roy, Pronay. Interview with Dalai Lama. NDTV. 1 April, 2008.

7

Reign of Terror and Dilemma in Asif Currimbhoy's *Inquilab (Revolution)*

Though several plays have been written in India dealing with a variety of social issues, there are very few who have written plays which can be stage produced. This is where Asif Currimbhoy (1928-1975) has his singular position by producing realistic plays for the stage.

He deal with serious social, political, moral and religious issues with pathos, sentiment, irony and social criticism Currimbhoy is considered India's first authentic voice in theatre writing plays of dissent (Bowers viii). All his issues, though local in colour, are of universal appeal, drawing attention to problems of man everywhere such as denial of human rights, justice and freedom. This is evident from the appreciation he has received from theatres across the world, where the plays have been successfully staged. The conflicts presented are internal as well as external in nature, rendering them superb psychological studies.

The dramatist explores universal human predicament through his social, moral, religious and political concerns in the plays. He is a voice of universal revolt and anguish. And it is compassion that unifies his plays (Currimbhoy ix). Sensing conflicts everywhere he says, "...conflict in theatre, conflict at every level – physical, mental, emotional – because from the time really you meet with other people, what is called human relationships" (Rajinder).

Inquilab, *The Refugee* and *Sonar Bangla,* clubbed together as Bengal trilogy, are set in the background of the Naxalite revolt that haunted West Bengal; the refugee problem faced by the state in the wake of unrest in the freedom struggle for Bangladesh; and the Indo-Pak war. In these plays, K.R. Srinivasa Iyengar finds that the playwright has scrutinised the basic human condition and portrayed the agonised expression of his social conscience (Currimbhoy iii).

Inquilab while depicting the Naxalite struggle in Bengal, probes into the way violence breaks loose. The play is an assessment of the Naxal movement grew powerful in Calcutta in the 1970s.

It was Charu Majumdar who established the Communist Party of India (Marxist-Leninist) and organized several armed risings of landless agricultural labourers, especially in eastern India in 1967. It came to be known as Naxalite Movement named after the village of Naxalbari in West Bengal, where it first began. Eventually it developed into an urban guerrilla movement, especially in Calcutta. Its programme of terror was suppressed with considerable violence. The CPI (M-L) eventually split up into several factions, one of which adopted a policy of participating in constitutional politics, but Naxalite atrocities continued into the early 1990s ("Naxalite Movement." http://www.encyclopedia.com).

The objective of the movement was seizure of power through an agrarian revolution. The strategy was to eliminate feudal order to free the poor from the oppression of landlords, bringing about land reforms. They employed guerilla warfare by the peasants to eliminate the landlords and build up resistance against the state's police force which assisted the landlords. The Naxalbari revolt was crushed by the police within a few months, however, it unleashed a flow of events which escalated over the years into a political movement that brought about far-reaching changes in India's socio-cultural scene. In spite of crushing the movement, Naxalism as an ideology has remained a great force with in India, due to feudal exploitation and oppression of the rural poor and the repressive Governmental policies to silence them ("Naxalbari." http://venus.unive). By the early 1970s, the Naxalite movement had spread to several parts of India - Andhra Pradesh, Kerala, Bihar Uttar Pradesh and Punjab. The alarming situation forced the Government to investigate into its causes. The committee set up compiled its report in 1969 entitled *The Causes and Nature of Current Agrarian Tensions*, and acknowledged: "The basic cause of unrest, namely, the defective implementation of laws enacted to protect the interests of the tribals, remains...unless this is attended to, it would not be possible to win the confidence of the tribals whose leadership has been taken over by the extremists" ("Naxalbari." http://venus.unive). By 1972, Naxalite rebellion was put down with the capture of the ideologue Charu Mazumdar from a Calcutta hideout on July 16, 1972. Though he died in police custody 12 days after his arrest, the movement continued even after his death with occasional encounters between the police and the Naxalites in villages in Andhra Pradesh, Bihar West Bengal and other states ("Naxalbari." http://venus.unive). Though the movement has been suppressed, its ideology will continue to threaten the Indian ruling powers as long as they fail to address the misery and social oppression of the poorest of the poor in India.

In *Inquilab* Currimbhoy takes us through three main scenes – a classroom, a prayer room and a Bengali countryside. For the dramatist "The play is the nightmare and the redemption of today's Calcutta…Amidst all the uncertainties…" (Bowers 7).

The play opens with the classroom scene where Datta, a professor of law, in his 50s with a conservative, old worldish British approach, lecturing to his alert, intelligent and restless students. In the crowd is also his son, Amir. He speaks to the students in the background of the ensuing Durga Puja vacation. He reminds them to introspect on the socio-political situations in his "dying city" Calcutta besieged by social maladies.

> Perhaps…this is the time for… reflection over the past… Impatient? Let us not get carried away, young men. Difficult times, I admit Culcutta, my Culcutta, a "dying city"? Processions? Strikes? Gheraos? Violence? Bandhs? Breakdown of law and order? Revolt Naxal revolt, my friends? Slogans of Gandhi or Mao?... Are there bombs in your head or brains, gentlemen? I hear… there are some amongst you… the tyranny of the minority I call it… who question these holy institutions of learning, like our holy mother Durga (Currimbhoy 10).

It is a predicament that the professor finds difficult to sort out, though he remains firm in pointing out the tyranny of the minority.

Provoked by his lecture, some students resort to banging the desk with fists, rulers and chappals. A frenzied crowd keeps shouting slogans, "CLASS ENEMIES MURDABAD! JOTEDARS MURDABAD! POLICE MURDABAD! INQUILAB! INQUILAB ZINDABAD!" (11). A distraught professor sits alone looking at the portrait of Mahatma Gandhi and soliloquies: "Gandhiji… Gandhiji…

how to make them understand that non-violence is an active philosophy? That it was used by you to fight violence" (11). He is heart broken as even his own son has turned against him.

Soon Amar enters and argues with his father on proletarian internationalism, calling himself a revisionist. He pinpoints his passionate cause of the poor dying of hunger due to the undue divide between rich and poor. He challenges his father. "And you talk of EDUCATION, father! Institutes of education that have now shackled us for generations and generations. What for?...I ask? So that there can be more unemployed millions? So that your bourgeois hierarchy remains intact! So that you've doped the masses sufficiently into complacency and resignation? You can have it..., but don't stuff it down our throat! You were the Gods that failed, father!.. I belong... to the cause... of the revolution... and my guru...outside" (14). Such strong anti-establishment sentiments expressed by his own son is a shocking revelation of how far indoctrination can lead to even breaking familial ties.

The sequence moves to Professor speaking to his wife who is busy decorating the statue of Durga for the celebrations. They talk of their elder son who was lost and perhaps dead in Mizoram due to his revolutionary activities. They are now worried about their younger son Amar who has gone on the wrong track believing in Naxalite ideology. This is a very painful predicament Professor and his wife undergoes.

The scene shifts to the puja meal at the Professor's house for which zamindar Jain and his daughter Suprea are present. Jain speaks of his trouble with his labourers who have been like part of his household, consider him a capitalist. The professor tells him that he is "A pacifist for maintenance of an existing order. An order of vested interests" (18). Amar, on the contrary, speaks out his revisionist views, "Land to the landless. Collective farming. Community holdings. A distribution of surplus land to be done immediately" (18). Amar begins to challenge Jain with disrespect, " We'll grab the land, old man, because the young like me are impatient and hungry. Then there'll be no distinction between the good and the bad landlord, because being landlord is bad enough! (19). An infuriated Jain reaffirms that the land belongs to him, received from his forebears, where he worked day and night to produce from it. As Amar walks away, Supreya tries to cool him with her flirting, but he calls her a temptress and a spy. Back home, Amar awaits the arrival of a friend, Ahmed, who he calls his guru.

Next scene shifts to the class room where some student naxalites gather in the night. The meeting is conducted by Ahmed. He tells that a revolutionary theory without revolutionary practice is of no avail. He calls for an armed struggle by the peasants to introduce socialist revolution to replace parliamentary democracy. He chalks out the four commandments of the peasant revolution: "One we must go among the masses and concern ourselves with their weal and woe. Two, the mobilization of the people will create a vast sea in which to drown the enemy. Three, seem to come from the east but attack from the west...avoid the solid, attack the hollow... deliver a lightning blow, seek a lightning decision. Four: the only way to final victory is the strategy of protected war" (25-6). He further establishes Mao's slogan that it is necessary to bring about a brief reign of terror in every rural area. He exhorts them to combine persuasion, terror and aid and to organize Peasants Union, the Krishak Sabha with weapons of combs, spears, knives and sickles.

The action shifts to the village farm-land and to a peasant's home where a clandestine meeting of peasants takes place with a young Naxalite organizer who is a student of Ahmed. In the course of the discussion the young man tells them that they toil for the damned greedy zamindars who exploit them, giving them only hunger, disease and death in return. One of the villagers tells him that their zamindar is not a tyrant. He works with them and they do not starve due to any exploitation. The villager also brings to his attention that they are not ignorant about ceilings on land holdings as the Socialist State Government keeps informing them of reforms through the political workers. The young revolutionary is told by the peasants to go back to the city and learn more before teaching them. A certain Shomik points out that both sides are right. He gives solution to their predicament, inciting them to grab land. However, he justifies that liberation has to be through revolt. According to him their landlord Jain is just, but he points out, "But he's working on our land and not we on his! We want our law! Not the landlord's, and not the Government's!" (17). Shomik requests the Maoists to lend their hand to fight together.

The sequence moves to Shomik's home where he talks with his wife Sarala, telling her that he is involved in righting the wrong fighting for equality. But his wife objects to his plans as she wants him to protect and give security to his home. He retorts saying what he wants is self-respect and freedom. He longs to take revenge on the zamindars who have subjugated the peasants into slaves. He wants to take up the cause of the downtrodden being their leader.

On the other side of the house, the sequence shifts to zamindar Jain and Devdas the politician visiting Shomik's father and his blind mother. Jain complains about Dada's fiery son who has become a leader. He gives some money to Dada for his wife's treatment. They ask Dada to call his son Shomik. As he arrives, Shomik forcefully takes out the money given to his father. Devdas speaks of the law and order problems faced by the Government when people resort to violence, which in turn need eradication through force. He tells Shomik to be practical and work for his party. Showmik, instead, asks for a land of his own to cultivate. Meanwhile, Ahmed and Amar arrive. They are introduced to the politician and the zamindar. Devdas warns Shomik of his association with the revolutionaries. "You've gone too far, Shomik! I warn you... You're in this gooda-gang...I'll remember all of you!" (37). Devdas and Ahmed have met each other in the midst of violence. Ahmed reminds him of his greed in the name of socialism. Ahmed reminds him how he sent para-military to Mizoram to kill one single revolutionary, leading a revolution. Hearing this Devdas leaves.

Amar and Ahmed exchange their views of the revolution. Amar points out that they are giving too much emphasis to the villages, instead he opines that the unrest should begin from the industrial complexes with strikes, lockouts, bundhs and gheraos. Shomik on the other hand wants the revolution to strike roots in the rural areas and spread all over the country. Ahmed upholds both the views as revolution carries no individual ideology. He calls on each one to work out the revolution in their different areas of work – in the class room, field and factory. His search is for the ultimate "the cause and the effect. The cycle of generations that revolt. The great burning desire within us that is prepared to kill and recreate. Build the new world that is as close to God's image as Man is ...It's all here. In the seed" (40). This is a symbolic statement on the seed of a revolution bringing in destruction and further leading to construction of a new social order.

Act II opens with Professor Datta lecturing to his students about the turn of events. He doesn't approve of the morality of land grabbing. He gives his legal opinion on the matter that land grabbing is an attack on the fundamental right. "under article 31, no person can be deprived of his property save by the authority of law" (41). The students show their indifference as teletype messages appear :CLASS ENEMIES MURDABAD...INQUILAB...INQUILAB ZINDABAD (41).

The scene shifts to a field where two peasants discuss the crisis situation. One suggests that if they join the movement they could also become landlords. His friend is of the opinion that they could also land up in jail. They realize that they are in a dilemma, caught between the devil and the deep sea. But they are worried "where to stop... how far to go. When the leadership is in the hands of extremists, ... it may not stop with the land grab" (43).

The scene shifts to the college corridor where the students are in discussion on the revolutionary views. One of the boys warns not to be carried away as, "Being a Naxal sympathizer is not being a Naxal. A lot of us in college are sympathizers...not all of it political" (44). One of the girls point out that 23 years after independence politicians have been perpetuating British colonialism. The diverse opinions leave them in a situation of dilemma.

The scene shifts to a prison where two prisoners are being interrogated by an officer. One of them looks like a goonda. The police inspector warns them of dire consequences. The sequence gives a peep into criminality that reveals its ugly face in the wake of a revolution.

The scene further shifts back to the story of the cultivable field. A group of peasants are there armed with lathis, spears and sickles. They are very assertive as they make the land grab. Shomik, their leader, points to a spear and warns any one who would dare to remove it. They don't care for anyone, be it the politician Devdas or zamindar Jain, who have been a party to the perpetuation of the oppressive system. He further asserts "We are taking the law into our own hands... because this is the only law that produces results!... The measurements of land are complete... each one equal share.. I want landlord Jain to share alike... If he resists...we shall have to try him out, according to our own laws" (50). The matter is to be tried in their Courts and Councils of Justice. The crowd keeps shouting slogans in collective threat.

There is a quick transition back to the college scene with sound of sudden explosion of a bomb on the road at the college campus. The screaming students keep running for safety. Amar is seen dashing up to Supra. Holding her hands, he tells her to warn her father of the danger he faces if he resists the land grabbing peasants.

As the scene moves to Professor's residence, he is seen very disturbed as he awaits the arrival of his son Amar. After a while, Ahmed walks in to tell him to inform the police to search for Amar. The professor lets out his angst as Amar has been accused of having connection with the police slaying in the blast. Ahmed points out how the Professor is in conflict with his son. He acknowledges that they were both poles apart as father and son. However, he is convinced that his son is not guilty of any crime as he is too weak inside.

The next scene takes place in the field at night where the Council of Justice is holding its meeting to try landlord Jain who is tied up in the centre. Ahmed nominates Shomik as the prosecutor. Amar demands an honest trial. However, he is accused of being a friend of the landlord. Amar pleads with the council to give a fair judgment as Jain has been fair in his dealings, working hard on his land. Shomik does not accept his opinion as Jain belongs to the privileged class, having loyalty to his own people. Hence, he is to be judged as a class enemy. Shomik accuses Amar to be a defector, since he protects his father's friend as defence counsel. Shomik is willing to consider the case if Jain is willing to repent. Amar tries to convince jain to surrender, pleading guilty. But he remains unrelenting.

The scene shifts to politician Devdas found in the company of a police inspector and a big-wheel politician from the Centre. They are alarmed at the prevailing lawless situation, yet are trying to make maximum political mileage from the grim situation. The Bin-wheel politician threatens Devdas of the possibility of President's Rule. Devdas demands that he is not stripped of his position. As they discuss, Suprea comes all excited, searcing for her father. They all accompany the girl to the field. Mesmeric teletape on wall appears,

"RED TERROR...BATTLE OF ANNIHILATION... CHAIRMAN MAO... DEATH TO CLASS ENEMIES...JOTEDAR MURDABAD...ZAMINDAR MURDABAD" (65). Suprea's shattering scream is heard as Jain's severed head appears hung on two poles.

Act II opens a few months latter with the scene of Professor Datta and Ahmed standing on two separate daises in the classroom. It is a meeting of the hardened inner-core-of Naxalite-students-in-clandestine-nighttime-meeting. The are to judge if Amar is a defector or a loyalist. The student leaders accuse Amar for having defended Jain who happens to be his father's friend.

The scenes shift in quick successions to Shomik's old blind mother and Amar's grieving mother. Focus is shifted to the politician Devdas and the Big-wheel politician in discussion. After a blackout we find Shamik bidding farewell to his wife Sarala. He tell her not to worry as he is going on his mission with the revolution.

Suprea and Amar appear on scene. Amar sympathises with her having lost her father. He was helpless in his attempts to save his life.

> SUPREA; And yet you didn't do anything to stop it.
> AMAR: I couldn't do anything to stop it...You must believe me.
> SUPREA: ...my father looked upon you as his son. Felt that one day... we'd be married,
> and that you'd carry on the tradition.
> AMAR: We will. We will, Suprea.
> SUPREA: But you don't believe in marriage or traditions...you believe in causes,
> and martyrdom... and endless suffering.
> ...
> AMAR: There's something merciless about a cause...There is something wrong in our
> society, your teaching – just as there was something wrong in the way your
> father...
> was killed...when I tried to save your father...I almost had it there.
> SUPREA: Then why do you persist in this madness?

> AMAR: because… I'm coming close… from a pull…in opposite directions. My mind and
> heart are taxed… to the extreme. The next… will be the most revealing.
> The ultir ›ıte test of loyalty and guilt.
> SUPREA: Are you going… to hurt more people… to prove things to yourself (75-6).

Amar's predicament makes him loose his sense of proportion. He is a mentally deranged person struggling in between a to be or not to be situation.

After a blackout, the scene returns to Professor Datta who stands alone in the library rearraging the statue of his venerated Sir Asutosh. Suddenly a group of Naxal students, led by Amar, invade the room shouting slogans to "OVERTHROW!...FILTHY BOURGEOIS LANDLORD UNIVERSITY! BOURGEOIS LANDLORD GOVERNMENT! REVISIONIST EDUCATION! REVISIONIST PROFESSOR!" (77). He requests the students to protest without violence being rational and constitutional. As the commotion continues a piercing scream is heard and the boys setting ablaze the library. Seeing Amar, Professor attempts in vain to calls him, but he pretends not to pay heed to him. They break down the statue of Asutosh. As Amar observes a boy push down his father, he threatens to kill him if he dared touching again.

Amar is appointed prosecutor carry out verdict in the execution of the statue of Sir Asutosh. Axe in hand he breaks apart the marble head of the statue, as though hypnotised by the fury of the crowd. The Professor, lying on the floor, staggers up. In the semi darkness he could see Ahmed holding a sickle coming forward. With a jerk he buries into Professor's back as he embraces him.

Act II scene II takes place a few months later. Amar tells Ahmed that though he believes in the socialist revolution, he disagrees with their methods. He feels his father's approach was right, "that change should come through the will of the majority…expressed through a free vote" (80). He feels guilty for his father's death. Ahmed convinces him that it all happened after Naxal raid. Amar feels that he has betrayed the cause. But Ahmed points out his outlook: "The cause is larger than either of us. And each of us still continues to follow it differently" (81). He further says Shomik is becoming a great leader and one day both he and Amar might differ in the methods employed in executing social justice. Ahmed speaks out his idea of revolution that brings life from death. "We were all caught in the vortex of struggle. Each of us searched the ultimate in our own emancipation… Yes, mine had turned full circle…People, events, this life, meant nothing to me…There is the harsh inevitability about it, the struggle for birth, for survival, where one has to kill to live again" (81). As the scene fades out, Suprea is heard calling Amar as Ahmed stands alone. Meantime from the balcony of Professor Datta's house his wife comes with a tray of rice from which she picks up a healthy seed and flings it into the fertile ground as Ahmed looks on.

The revolution takes its toll. Datta is killed by his own son's colleague who is a Naxal extremist. Jain the landlord is another victim of violence. Finally Amar comes to the realization that his father was right in upholding the Gandhian principles: "…my father was right…that change should come through the will of the majority…expressed through a free vote…I've found my path…and it will be the same as that of my father" (80-1).

The play ends symbolically with Ahmed confirming his stand of pursuing his Marxist revolution, while Prof. Datta's wife observing Ahmed, picks up healthy rice seeds from a tray and flings into fertile soil. The play pictures the futility of Marxist ideology bringing destruction through revolution.

As one reads *Inquilab,* the characters leap off the page and seize by the throat. "The canvas Currimbhoy paints here is one massive dilemma composed of a hundred small ones – 'the devil and the deep.' "(Bowers 7). Various predicaments are presented in the play such as : i) The peasants caught between – to join or not to join the revolution; ii) The politician's involvement to suppress the rebellion or bring in President's rule; iii)The wife of Shomik reminding him of choosing between his dreams. All he wanted was to possess a piece of land, but now he dreams of leading a national revolution. He forgets his ideals and takes up to violence with different motives; iv) Datta while lecturing on Gandhian ways, questions the new wave of revolution; v) Execution of Jain and the mockery of the court of justice; vi) Amar's continuous dilemma leading to destruction; vii) Predicament of Suprea after her father was killed by the revolutionaries. She still believes in Amar. Her love transforms him

viii) Ahmed's double face – a friend and assassin of Professor whom he embraces to death; ix) Who is right? The Constitutionalists or the Revolutionaries. The Constitutionalists dream of a welfare state while the Naxals believe in establishing a classless society; x) Final sequence of Ahmed determined to continue pursuing the revolution and Professor's wife throwing the grain, as though it is like the fulfilment of Ahmed's statement: "The great burning desire within us that is prepared to kill and recreate. Build the new world that is as close to God's image as Man is ...It's all here. In the seed" (40).

Finally, Amar realizes that his revolutionary outlook will not bring about the utopian dream of social justice. His father was right and he should have listened to that mature voice. Only democratic rule of the people, by the people and for the people built on a secular corruption free society can usher in a final solution.

Currimbhoy believes in social realism and *Inquilab* is his thesis to prove it (Reddy 35). It is the character of Amar that strikes a balance in between the two positions of Constitutionalism and proletarian internationalism. In the beginning he stands in contrast to his father who stood for peace and stability through non-violent methods, but violence and bloodshed makes him give up Naxalism. In *Inquilab* the playwright affirms that the Naxal shortcut is no happy solution to any problem and that evil and hatred can be overcome only through love and understanding (Reddy 52).

Currimbhoy's plays are all centred on human predicament which puzzles him so much that he shares the pain and agony of humanity through the characters he creates. The pathetic human condition is uppermost in his mind. His imagination is built on the experience of life. There is a perfect fusion of thought and feeling as "the world of the mind as well as the social and political world that surround him... He has something to say... a message to deliver, a vision to fulfil and he must work, speak, write and act" (Meserve 10).

However, Scholars like M.K. Naik have pointed out certain incongruities in his work and art:

> Most of these plays have a strong 'documentary' element about them and there is no attempt to understand and project in dramatic terms the ideological implications of the political conflicts dealt within. The dramatist appears to be primarily interested in the thrill of the exciting events rather than the thought

> processes which shaped them. The result is sheer reportage; and when Currimbhoy gives free rein to his imagination, the upshot is often crude and contrived symbolism... Unless Currimbhoy realizes that drama is something more than simply play of lights, plethora of sounds and parade of violence, all his enviable industry and enthusiasm are unlikely to produce viable and worthwhile plays (Naik 258-61).

Despite the flaws pointed out, his plays have been highly appreciated and successfully staged in several countries. A perceptive critic will also find it extremely difficult to separate his didacticism from his dramatic art. His dramatic techniques are meant "to provide visual images to stimulate the minds, the ears, and the eyes of his audience" (Meserve 15). In the process he makes excellent use of monologues, choruses, pantomime, music and visual effects.

Currimbhoy's compassion for humanity is the central motif as he details out the predicament of man in agony and ecstasy. His purpose is to make his audience/readers appreciate life in its totality. In the process he presents social evils and chaos letting his audience/readers to find the right answers themselves. At the same time one gets the impression that the playwright is personally involved in the plays and uses the stage to present societal issues with the intention of social transformation.

Works Cited

Bowers, Faubion et al. *Appreciations of Asif Currimbhoy*. Calcutta: Writers Workshop, 1975.

Currimbhoy, Asif. *Inquilab*. 2nd ed. Calcutta: Writers Workshop, 1993.

Meserve, Ruth & Walter Meserve. "Foreword." *The Hungry Ones*. Calcutta: Writers Workshop, 1992.

Naik, M.K. *A History of Indian English Literature*. New Delhi: Sahitya Akademi, 1982.

"Naxalbari." http://venus.unive.it/asiamed/eventi/schede/naxalbari.html(1967):THE NAXALITE MOVEMENT IN INDIA.

"Naxalite Movement." http://www.encyclopedia.com/doc/1O48-

Rajinder, Paul & Jacob Paul. *Enact*. Interview with Currimbhoy. December. 1970.

Reddy, P. Bayapa. *The Plays of Asif Currimbhoy*. Calcutta. Writers Workshop,1985.

8

Social Degradation in Asif Currimbhoy's *The Dissident M.L.A*

Currimbhoy explores universal human predicament through his social, moral, religious and political concerns in his plays. He is a voice of universal revolt and anguish. And it is compassion that unifies his plays (Currimbhoy 1993a:ix). Sensing conflicts everywhere he says,'...conflict in theatre, conflict at every level – physical, mental, emotional – because from the time really you meet with other people, what is called human relationships' (Rajinder, Jacob. December1970).

All his issues, though local in colour, are of universal appeal, drawing attention to problems of man everywhere such as denial of human rights, justice and freedom. This is evident from the appreciation he has received from theatres across the world, where the plays have been successfully staged. The conflicts presented are internal as well as external in nature, rendering them superb psychological studies.

Based on the political events that took place in Gujarat in 1974, *The Dissident M.L.A.* centres on the evil designs of Manubhai to topple the Government. The play depicts various incidents such as students' protest against raise in mess bill at the Engineering college hostel, tough examinations, corrupt Government etc. The agitating students gherao the Vice Chancellor and publicly humiliate the Home Minister, shaving his head, blackening his face and parading him riding on a donkey. The events finally lead to dissolution of the Gujarat Assembly. The play is a social criticism in which the playwright satirises politicians who are corrupt and greedy

After Chimanbhai Patel became the chief minister of Gujarat in 1973, he drew protest from students and teachers over rampant corruption prevalent in the state. By and by, student protests grew due to high mess bills and poor quality of food in hostels, sparking off agitation in Ahmedabad in December 1973. The clashes between the police and students led to the formation of a students' committee known as the Nav Nirman Yuvak Samiti. To voice their grievances, an indefinite strike was called from 7 January 1974 in schools and colleges. They demanded reduction in educational fees, more campus facilities, distribution of quality food and arrest of black marketeers. It inspired Jayaprakash Narayan to launch the "total revolution" movement, the outcome of which was the Emergency and not a resurgence of public morality. Widespread riots in January led to imposition of curfew in 44 towns rocking the whole state. Dissident leaders of the ruling party also openly supported the agitation which demanded the resignation of Patel. Indira Gandhi was forced to ask Patel to step down on February 9. By March, students had got 95 of 167 MLAs to resign. Morarji Desai, leader of Congress (O), went on an indefinite fast in support of the demand. On March 16, the assembly was dissolved and President's rule imposed. In the beginning, Nav Nirman, was a buzz word for students and their mentors. But their value system was no different from the politicians they were combating and the agitation had no effect on arresting corruption. Patel became chief minister again with BJP support in 1990. Eventually, Nav Nirman provided ground for reactionary forces to flourish ("Nav Nirman"http:/ indiatoday.intoday.in).

The illustration below shows how Manubhai takes the central stage with all others as his satellites, to bring to fulfilment his political ambition. Even the donkey is given a position as a character, which is symbolic of the unintelligent life he lives.

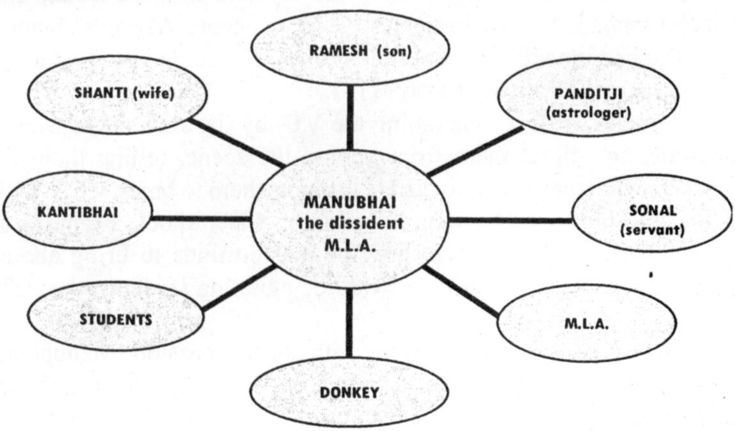

The play opens with Manubhai restlessly pacing up and down in his living room awaiting the arrival of his only son Ramesh. He is a dissident M.L.A. in his mid-forties, who has gulped down several times from the half-empty bottle of Scotch, to spend the tension filled night. He keeps grumbling and cursing his son who has not arrived. Meanwhile voice of his wife could be heard uttering evil of her husband: "That useless father of yours, Ramesh…Grow up and disgrace him…He'll try to shine through you, my noble, beautiful boy. But… you…down! He sucked the life out of me. Don't let him escape!" (*DMLA* 9). Manu expresses his disgust for her wanting his son never to listen to her, a frustrated, brainless woman. Her taunting voice can be heard, deriding her husband who she predicts will be wrecked in his political career. Manu, ignoring her wretched nature, writhes in frustration, longing for his son's return. Soon he could hear Ramesh call him out from the dark, refusing to come to light if his father doesn't agree to his demands.

Ramesh doesn't want his father take advantage of him with his tricks for his political gains. Manu assumes that his son has come to consult him on their strategy to continue with the student agitation. Ramesh counts the various reasons for the student unrest such as raise in the mess fees of L.P. Engineering College and the rampant corruption in the examination system. Manu is also told that since he is the dissident M.L.A. that the students need his direction as he is well versed in his old tricks in the trade. He, on his part, also advises Ramesh to go for the big ones in the system like the Dean, the Principal and the V.C. He instigates: "…Try a gherao. A simple gherao. One of those innoculous non-violent ones. I'll guide you. Listen to my whispers. Follow what I say" (13).

The scene shifts to gheraoing the V.C. by the students as Manu continues to direct them from behind the scene, telling them in whispers what they ought to do. He prompts them to break V.C's will and shame him until he wets his pants in sheer shock. Manu as a dissident M.L.A. is shown how he masterminds to bring about political instability in the state, with the agitating students, through his son.

When he returns home, heaving with unspent passion, Manubhai, goes straight to his astrologer to force out a lucky forecast of his political future. He is advised to control his passion for food, wine and women. But a reckless Manu has set his mind on his planned insurrection in the Legislative Assembly the following day.

Scene 4 brings to focus proceedings in the Legislative Assembly, where the Speaker is unable to control a rude and agitated assembly. Manubhai imposingly speaks out with suddenly screaming profanities, "This Government needs to be pulled down, and this Assembly dissolved. NONE OF YOU WOULD GET RE-ELECTED AND YOU KNOW IT!" (18). In his anger, he throws his chappals at them causing a general pandemonium.

As Manubhat returns home, the episode exposes his sexually perverse life, having an affair with Sona, the servant girl, rescued from the Rescue Home where she used to be molested by the Minister for Social Welfare. The condition of Rescue Homes for women is portrayed ironically by the dramatist as centres of sexual exploitation by politicians in the name of social work, though set up with social concern by Gandhians like Kantibhai.

In act 2, donning his Gandhian outfit, Manu visits his political mentor, Kantibhai. He appraises him of the way the agitating students and the women, continue to spearhead, with devotion and self-sacrifice, like the Salt March by the Mahatma. Kantibhai hails it as done with moral courage in national interest. Manubhai sympathises with his mentor, being shabbily treated, though he was a force in the old party. He points out how moral courage has slackened, generating strikes, gheraos and morchas instead of nation building, which was the prime motive of freedom fighters like him. He terms violence generated by the students merely by a bunch of hooligans. When he questions Manu about the recent happenings in the legislative assembly, he fumbles for a suitable reply. Kantibhai reminds him of the need for moral rectitude and Brahmacharya to generate moral fibre in society. Manu tries to wind up his courtesy call, flattering Kantibhai, who led selfless non-cooperation movement through fasting and peaceful ways.

Returning home, Manubhai gulps down scotch to drown his shame, exposed by Kantibhai. He turns grumpy and curses the old man for his moral fibre when the Government has been corrupt to the core. Meanwhile, Sonal comes in to clean the floor, making sexual signals to him. Putting off the candle, he tiptoes towards her and indulges in sex. Hearing the braying of the donkey and the presence of his wife around, he abruptly stops it, telling her to be off. Moments later Shanti approaches him with a peg of whisky and tries to make love to him. He desists her passionate approach wanting to have sex with him. He makes excuses saying that Kantibhai had advised abstinence.

Following morning, as Manubhai wearily drinks a glass of milk, Ramesh comes in with a group of students, wanting to have a private meeting to discuss their further strategies. They plan to begin their clean movement called Nav Nirman Samiti with "no interference, no trade unions, no opposition parties, no money-businessmen" (33). They assess their success in gheraoing the V.C and making the Minister ride on a mule.

Manubhai keeps exhorting the students to continue the agitation with a little more organised action and a tinge of violence to make it effective. He wants a total bandh to paralize the state aiming to bring down the Government and the Chief Minister.

The episode moves to the pandemonium created by the students crying in the streets with Manubhai yelling, "...Burn the fair price shops!... Catch the food-grain sellers...Beat up the black marketeers. The only language they understand is fear!... Hijack those buses! Bring the trains to a halt! Burn those milkbooths down!" (34). Being provoked, the students go about burning and looting in the streets. When things go out of hand, some students begin to question the movement. "What are we doing? Have we ever stopped to question ourselves? Or are we just getting caught in a madness" (35). But Manubhai keeps inspiring the students not to lose sight of their main objective of getting the downfall of the corrupt body. When Ramesh tells his father that things are getting out of control, blaming him for using the students for his selfish mad motives, Manubhai merely blames them for asking for his help. He continues to justify his stand: "We are not offenders. We're creating new laws in a free society by breaking old ones. Killing? We've had nothing to do with it. They've killed one of mine... We won't take it lying down. We'll kill too. Rally around!...Attack every Government building! Burn every Police Station! Burn! Loot! Kill!" (38).

The sequence shifts to meeting of the Congress High Command that condemns Manubhai being guilty of indiscipline and anti-party activities. He pleads not guilty being a committed party worker. When he questions corruption and price rise and political rivalry, he is dismissed from the party. Next sequence leads Manubhai in the house of Kantibhai, seeking sympathy for having encouraged the use of violence as a means to an end. Kantibhai tells him of God's conscience besides man's conscience: "And God's conscience is greater: it forms the basis of Natural Law. Man's law may be broken, but not the Natural Law" (39).

The scene ends as Ramesh returns home to inform his father that the Ministry has resigned and the C.M. has stepped down. But his father is not satisfied with the news, as he wants the dissolution of the Legislative Assembly.

Act 3 introduces the scene at the Legislative Assembly where the Governor reads in the house the Presidential Order. Manubhai misbehaves in the Assembly and objects to the suspended animation of the Assembly. He demands dissolution of the house. As the Governor disregards the demand, all the opposition M.L.A.s walk out making it appear like a voluntary dissolution, though the Congress High Command had warned party M.L.As not to leave.

The students, on their part, take full credit for their movement without the politicians, trade unionists and mill owners' involvement with their vested interests. Their heated discussions wind up with an introspection by Ramesh: " Comrades, we've revolted against corruption… And it seemed to us corruption came only with politicians and business men, hoarders and blackmarketeers… Well, there's another kind of corruption coming in too. The corrupt, unethical, power-hungry student. And what are you doing to stop that?" (45).

Scene three further depicts Manubhai's attempt at gathering more and more M.L.As to resign from the Assembly. He tells his wife how he has got 45 out of 108 members tender their resignation. He keeps on calling several M.L.A.s on telephone to get their resignation. Finding resistance from some, he becomes more abusive on phone. Meanwhile Shanti tells him about Kantibhai's announcement of his fast unto death until the Assembly is dissolved. Hearing the news, Manubhai becomes very crazy and starts laughing hysterically. Finding him going mad, Shanti slaps him to bring sanity. The comical section brings to focus how political ambitions can lead to such mad behaviour in people. Manubhai keeps grumbling about his mentor Kantibhai who has gone crazy, "Can't believe it! That descrepit old moralist going on fast unto death! Who does he think he is? Gandhi? What times does he think he's living in? Gandhian? The old fool! They will let him die...He's a spent force" (47). Immediately, he goes to meet Kantibhai to stop him from his fast unto death as it would be only seen as his taking revenge for having been thrown out of the Government.

The scene shifts to Manubhai snoring on the couch, humorously presenting him shouting, while apparently asleep: "You let that old man die and I'll see to it that you all fry in Delhi!" (50). Sonal walks in with her bundle planning to go back to Kantibhai, to look after him in his old age. Since his wife died she wanted to be with him to give some comfort in his loneliness as if to pay back her debt to him for having put her in the Rescue Home. Manubhai lusted to have her for a last time to satisfy his lust. When she refuses the M.L.A. sighs uttering , "I guess all good things come to an end. Good bye, love. Look after the old goat... the old man. If there's any trouble, call me" (52). Ironically, the sequence presents how corrupt both the men prove themselves to be, exploiting women in their own subtle ways in the name of humanitarian service.

In scene 7 Ramesh finds his father fully intoxicated, lying in his smoky room. He announces the happy news that the Assembly has been dissolved. But Kantibhai had not called off his fast in protest against Manubhai's call to protest in the streets. An argument ensues between the two in which important issues are analysed:

> MANU: True. I made you follow my will.
> RAMESH: Why?
> MANU: (*frowning, searching within himself*) I don't know. Maybe it was to liberate myself. To make you do all the things I failed to do myself in life.
>
> RAMESH (*angrily*) But what about me! My own feelings! Or didn't that matter?
>
> MANU: It was my love...
> RAMESH: It wasn't your love. It was your ego.
> MANU: I'm sorry. I couldn't differentiate.
> RAMESH: But I'm sure you thought it made a man out of me.
> MANU" Yes.
> RAMESH: Wrong again. I like to make my own timings, my own mistakes, to maturity. Not someone else's.

MANU: Where was the mistake? We... you and I... rooted out corruption.

RAMESH: Did we? You know what that wise old fox told me? He said there'd be a new election, and new corrupt M.L.A.'s would come in instead of the old corrupt ones... It means we've gone through all this for nothing. We'll have the same old corrupt Government as long as people live (54-5).

Manubhai laughs hysterically and goes off to the telephone to make appointment with Kantibhai to make him break his fast.

The play ends with Manubhai meeting his Astrologer to find out where his son is. He tells him of the destiny of man, "...we're both equally fallible. There really are no Absolutes in life...If I could be certain of it...Then I could believe that Man makes his own God" (55-6). As the Astrologer leaves, Manubhai lies on his couch and wearily closes his eyes. After a long pause he could be heard whispering with a quiver, "Ramesh. Oh how I pray God you return. I've never been so afraid in all my life" (56). The ghost of Ramesh appears, but he doesn't believe it to be his son. As he weeps in despair, the ghost leads him to the window to look out to the horizon to see his Ramesh "walking down the road" (56). Bursting out in grief he cries out "Ramesh! Ramesh! Yes, I see you there! Oh God, I've seen him! I'm certain now! And he's coming home!" (56).

Juxtapositioning the opening scene with the final sequence bring to light how social and familial disintegration takes place due to political manoeuvring, corruption and immorality. The opening scene depicting the restlessness of Manubhai, drinking and cursing his wife, expecting his son betray his political conniving. Ramesh refuses to come out of the dark if his father does not yield to his demands. Finally when the play ends, after having had all his plans executed through his son, Ramesh condemns him for his selfish motives. In the final sequence, Manubhai is a desperate man, haunted by the realization that he has lost his own son. Through satire and comedy, the dramatist draws attention to various factors that bring about disintegration of society through ambition, cunning and sexual pervasion.

The play focuses on the various issues that are a menace to social fabric, such as political corruption, student unrest and sexual perversion. In the final analysis, corruption continues in spite of change of guard in administration. Through the play Currimbhoy points out how idealistic youth are led astray by unscrupulous and corrupt politicians who channelise their youthful energy to create a sense of panic. He has also included violence and sex so rampant in our society, adding zest to the story.

Critics have pointed out certain incongruities in his work and art. Thought most of his plays have a strong 'documentary' element about them, he has not tried to understand and project in dramatic terms the ideological implications of the political conflicts dealt within. The dramatist seems to stress the thrill of the exciting events rather than the thought processes, thereby resulting in sheer reportage (Naik 258-60).

A perceptive critic will also find it extremely difficult to separate his didacticism from his dramatic art. His dramatic techniques are meant "to provide visual images to stimulate the minds, the ears, and the eyes of his audience" (Meserve 15). The play, through its comical and satirical device exposes avarice and corruption among politicians as well as the apparent idealism of students.

The play is an excellent study in human behaviour through dramatic devices such as the use of occasional dual scenes. It may be remarked that the playwright has very realistically presented a historical event with irony, satire and social criticism. Currimbhoy depicts social evils and chaos letting his audience/readers to find the right answers themselves, calling for introspection. At the same time one gets the impression that the playwright is personally involved in the plays and uses the stage to present societal issues with the intention of social transformation. However the playwright does not like to be labelled a propagandist as he claims to let his audience make their conclusions from his presentation of facts (Currimbhoy 1976 :41).

Works Cited

Currimbhoy, Asif. *The Dissident M.L.A.* Calcutta: Writers Workshop, 1974. (Abbreviated: *DMLA*).

—— *Inquilab*. 2nd ed. Calcutta: Writers Workshop, 1993a.

Meserve, Ruth & Walter Meserve. "Foreword." *The Hungry Ones*. Calcutta: Writers Workshop, 1992.

Naik, M.K. *A History of Indian English Literature*. New Delhi: Sahitya Akademi, 1982.

"NavNirman"http://indiatoday.intoday.in/site/Story/2727/COVER%20STORY/Pulse+of+the+people.

Rajinder, Paul & Jacob Paul. 1970. *Enact*. Interview with Currimbhoy. December.

9

Themes and Techniques in Sriranga's *Shadows in the Dark, Agnisakshi, Yama Vanquished* and *Ramarajya*

Adya Rangacharya (1904-1984) known as Sriranga was a great Sanskrit scholar and professor at Karnataka College, Dharward. Being fascinated by the rural stage in Kannada, professional theatre in Marathi, he had tried his hand at play-writing as a teenager. However it was from 1930 when he returned after his education in Britain, that he began writing plays under the influence of Shakespeare, Bernard Shaw and Ibsen. Committed to Gandhian ideology, he wrote 45 full length plays and over 60 short plays in Kannada (*SITD* 150).

In her introduction to *Shadows in the Dark: Four Plays by Sriranga*, Usha Desai noted the 'timelessness of the plays, the universality of his characters…and his deep understanding of human nature and the theatre.' (15). The great contribution of the playwright to Kannada theatre made Girish Karnard acknowledge him as the first Kannada playwright who 'mercilessly flayed social pretensions and created a language which younger playwrights could use.' (Ibid.8) Being a Gandhian he had his perception of political freedom calling for social change, leading to economic prosperity of India. His ideals called for a societal trasformation discarding casteism and religious fundamentalism.

His experiments with themes and techniques, with deeper analysis of human psychology, makes his apparently traditional dramatic form, excellent channel of social criticism. This paper is an attempt to examine the themes and techniques in his four translated plays *Shadows in the Dark, Agnisakshi, Yama Vanquished* and *Ramarajya.*

A brief understanding of *Natyashastra* may be of great help to understand the plays better. Sriranga himself recounts how it originated. 'Natya was created by Brahma... at the request of god's led by Mahendra as people of this world of pain and pleasures, goaded by greed and avarice and jealousy and anger, took to uncivilized ...ways of life. "Please give us something which would not only teach us but be pleasing both to eyes and ears...the Vedas are there but (some like) the Shudras are prohibited from listening to (learning from) them. Why not create for us a fifth Veda which would be accessible to all the Varnas (castes)?" Since Brahma knew Sudras were unable to practice it sincerely he entrusted it to Bharata and his sons. "So I practiced it with my sons, assigning each a fitting role, telling them where to stand and how to move, training them in words, emotions and movements' (12-14).

Bharata's *Natyashastra* in Sanskrit discusses ancient stage craft and various aspects of drama and it mirrored the essential and eternal India (Reddy 8). It is meant to entertain as well as to instruct and enlighten. It has given to Indian drama its form, objective and position in the social and cultural life of the people (Banker 37). The classical dramas were based on the epics and the Puranas. In course of time these declined to give way to folk theatre in many linguistic regions of India. Thus dramas began to be written in the vernaculars, some of which were translated into English in the past few years. In these translations there can be found a link between the east and the west, north and south, with Hindi, Marathi, Bengali and Kannada (Reddy 25). Many of these dramatists have attempted to retrieve ancient traditions by trans-historical inter-culturalism (35).

With British colonization there began the process of modernization, bringing about the encounter between east and west. As it has been pointed out, 'In contrast to the classical theatre, the folk theatre is characterized by its immediate accessibility by vitality and by its exuberance. They were regional, profane and secular as well. These Intermediary or Folk theatre represent the first phase of modernization' (Banker 1996:39). Some of the regional writers, being influenced by their western exposure, adopted western technique in their village theatre (40).

Critics like G.S. Shivarudrappa acknowledges the cultural influence of Sanskrit and western traditions in Kannada literature:

> Kannada did never reject Sanskrit, or submit itself completely to it, and moulded Sanskrit for its necessities.... Kannada has struggled with other languages. It has struggled, reacted and assimilated the other influences and has yet maintained its uniqueness. Our literature is one long record of the language's reaction to the influences of other Indian languages and the western literatures.... The reaction of Kannada to what is generally called as the Great tradition is noteworthy. Though Kannada has received its theme from the Great tradition, the themes so received have been re-worked to suit the local needs and requirements (Shivarudrappa 146-148).

Regional theatre is marked by its didacticism and socio-political commentary. A remarkable thing in the regional theatre is that, 'There is flexible concept of time and space and the ability to transform one space into many places...seeming mobility between spheres of realities; connectedness with the audience... maintaining a dialectical tension between the 'efficacious' and 'entertaining' tendencies' (Mukherjee 21-22).

Kannada theatre is both classical and folk based with noted playwrights such as T.P. Kailasam, K.V. Puttappa, D.R. Bendre, Adya Rangacharya and Shivarama Karanth. 'Kailasam and Sriranga brought on to the stage a heavy dose of realism. They portrayed the social problems that were plaguing the society of the day. They used satire and humour to set things right. They altered traditional structure of the play: music was given up, so also was the highly literary bookish language' (Banker 50).

For Sriranga *Natyashastra* was a Veda and his experiments and dramatic techniques were based on it (SITD:16). He was deeply influenced by the theatre of the absurd. The absurdists regarded themselves as loners and outsiders isolated in their private world. They were sensitive in projecting thoughts and feelings of their contemporaries. Their works were characterised by illogical situations, unconventional dialogue, and minimal plots to express the apparent absurdity of human existence and metaphysical anguish... According to them the true field of battle is inside us, in the Unconscious. Hence the theatre of the Absurd attacks us below the threshold of consciousness using mainly visual devices and language in a state of fragmentation. They mainly concern themselves with the doomed individual, the man in despair and distress, alone and bitter in the wide world (Sebastian 14-15).

1. Shadows in the Dark

As Sriranga himself had done research into the origin of Natyashastra, in *Shadows in the Dark,* he attempts to apply some of the dramatic techniques. It is a metadrama, a drama about drama, drawing attention to its own fictional status and attempting to make it successful on stage. It is a play about the process of play-writing with the theme of human predicament and irony of life.

The play begins with three persons discussing about play-writing. The 1st Person is a playwright who is asked by the other two persons to resume his play-writing. They insist on his writing plays that would appeal to an audience rather than to the reading public. They voice Srirangan's own conviction of having plays written for the stage than merely for sheer reading. The playwright is very emphatic when he refers to his vow never to write again. But the other two persons insist on his writing plays. Sriranga clearly states his stand in the debate that ensues that his plays are meant to be seen and not just read. Hence, mere reading the play can be the most unrewarding experience for any one as he employs stage techniques with justapositioning of episodes. The farcical element in the episodes is remarkable, yet there is lack of clear logical flow of events as in absurd theatre.

The conversation is interrupted by people shouting 'He's there! Catch him... ' and a policeman coming from behind the house and enquiring if they had noticed someone running away. The 1st Person (playwright) takes this as a cue and says, "That's the only thing missing in my play!" The three persons continue engaging in their conversation focussing on the nature of the play.

1st Person: What sort of a play?

2nd Person: A mythological play... What the public wants is a mythological play... Gods, demons, the court of India, the dances of Ranabha and Urvashi...

1st Person: ...Do you think that I am a small boy? Gods, demons, miracles – all these subjects appeal to the very young... What will the intellectuals say if I write such plays?... Do such things ever happen in everyday life?

2nd Person: That's the very reason why the public likes it, sir.

1st Person: No! When was it – in which ancient era – was it possible for one man to abduct his wife?

(*SITD* 24-25).

The conversation is interrupted by the earlier policeman who is looking for someone who has run away.

Policeman: Were you not saying that some man ran away with another's wife?

2nd Person: Havaldarsahib, he was telling us the story of a play.

Policeman: (*irritably*) If you are telling stories, please go inside and do it. Why do you come in the way of our work (25).

As they are engrossed in their exchange of views, a person who had run into the clump of trees creeps up and slips out. For the policeman the three persons telling stories have no relevance to reality. This is precisely why the two persons want the playwright to write plays on mythologies, making people live in a make-believe world. The juxtapositioning of sequences by the playwright generates the intended effect on the audience – mingling of art and life;, illusion and reality.

In the following sequence two rustics Malla and Mava enter, searching for Malla's son who has run away with someone's wife. Malla confesses that his son and the woman being deeply involved in love might have killed her husband. Malla leads Mava to his son's favourite hiding place in the clump of trees. The Policeman, a Citizen, Malla and Mava make their conjectures about the possible crime. Malla claims his son's innocence. The Citizen is convinced of a sex murder and alleges that he heard a woman's scream and concludes there should be two dead bodies around the clump of trees.

The Policeman questions the 1st Person (Playwright) if he had seen anybody near his house. But his interests are different as he is a playwright. The two Persons keep persuading the 1st Person to write a mythological play.

In the second act the Policeman enters reading two letters and exits. A uniformed chauffer enters followed by a young fashionable modern woman. They both look at each other in frustration and walk towards the clump of trees. As they exit the 1st, 2nd and 3rd Persons come on stage. The 1st Person is determined not to write any mythological play. The 2nd Person requests him to write a historical play as people would come to watch it. He suggests the plot about a king who is killed by his queen to get the kingdom and to continue her affair with the prince.

The discussion is interrupted by the arrival of the Policeman who excitedly takes out letters from his pocket containing information about the woman who had murdered her old husband. All absorbed in his work the policeman shows his annoyance with the three Persons who retire to the 1st Person's room to escape from the enquiries of the policeman.

The sequence that follows is that of the driver and the young woman. From their conversation it comes to light that she has run away from her old and rich husband to be with the driver with whom she is deeply involved. It was rumoured that the old man was murdered by the wife in connivance with the driver.

The next episode is of the Policeman in discussion with a Citizen who had earlier reported about the murder of a man by his wife. But the Policeman brings out a different report to the utter confusion of the Citizen. Meanwhile the young woman and the driver accuse each other of the crime. The Policeman is told by the Citizen of a car he spotted in the moonlight. Later the Citizen shouts from behind the trees that he had found the body of an old man who happened to be a sweet distributor.

The episode shifts to the three persons who emerge out of the house discussing the plot of the play where the wife kills the husband successfully. The juxtapositioning of the two episodes is remarkable. The drama in the making is proven to be a historical play, yet nothing is factual. The policeman interrogating the three persons whether they are discussing a play or acting in one, fuses the real and the imaginative – the action in the play on the one side and the process of writing a play on the other side. The absurd situation is remarkable in the dialogue that ensues.

In act III a young couple walk in and then exit. The Citizen emerges and from behind the house peeps at the couple. Expressing satisfaction and success he comes forward with a paper and places it at the rear of the stage under a stone.

The three persons emerge discussing on producing plays and staging them. The playwright has his arguments making the two persons request him to write any social plays about husband-wife relations and dealing with love, poverty and crime.

The Policeman arrives and interrupts the discussion showing his annoyance at their discussing crime in a play while he is on a criminal investigation of a man killed by his wife. He produces a note while the 2nd Person also brings out a similar note and begins to argue.

The episode that follows is that of the husband and the wife (the earlier young couple) discussing their fate. The husband suggests that they commit suicide hanging together on a tree. She accuses him of being a defeatist and objects to the suicidal plan. The conversation focus on the very concept of literature as imitation of life:

> **Policeman**: Why don't you go where they do all these things you are talking about, my man? Here...
>
> **Citizen**: All this happens in literature. This is why literature is so intensely emotional - and has this effect on us. If life is to be the same, we should see such things happen in life too. Then life would be imitating literature.
>
> **Policeman**: But they won't happen. After all, what do you think policemen are here for?
>
> ...
>
> 3rd **Person**: What is this? Is our Policeman also acting in a play? He is talking to himself.
>
> ...
>
> 1st **Person**: That is exactly what strikes me too!...But, who says anything these days? Anyway, what can they say? Are they capable of expressing their thoughts? They go and see a mythological play because they need not comment. They go for historical plays because adverse comments are not welcome. And now they say they prefer social dramas that require no comment whatsoever...In this world...until such a time as there are intelligent and sensitive people, I for one will not write plays. Nobody can do it. Darkness and Light, Night and day are the two basic truths in this world. The contrast and conflict between these two constitute the very essence of life. But when there are

no sensitive or discerning people, how do I create my characters or write plays?... (67-69).

The play is an excellent attempt in the absurd tradition. As Esslin Martin points out that the absurdists have no story or plot, no recognizable characters, no proper theme with a beginning and end. They reflect dreams and nightmares with incoherent babbling (Esslin 1968:21-22).

2. *Agnisakshi*

Agnisakshi is a dark tragedy which draws our attention to tendency in human nature to cause pain. The play revolves around the families of Sripati and Sarasu. The playwright has set three central characters each in the families.

Family of Sripati	**Family of Sarasu**
Sripati : a young man	**Sarasu** : a young woman
Rangannaraya : Sripati's father	**Amma** : Sarasu's mother
Atte : Rangannaraya's sister	
(aunt of Sripati)	**Mama** : Amma's brother
(Sarasu's uncle)	

These characters can be contrasted with each other in male/female order Sripati/Sarasu; Rangannaraya/Amma; Atte/Mama. The rest of the characters are Sripati's four friends and three youth who are members of the Anti Dowry Sangha. Sripati and Sarasu are to be married. But Sripati is adamant that his family shouldn't accept any dowry in the form of presents as he is the president of the Anti Dowry Sangha. The playwright has employed an excellent dramatic technique presenting both the families on stage side by side.

As the play begins the parents of Sripati and Sarasu are seated on stage in their respective homes. Action begins when the girl turns her face away from her mother in tears and wipes them while the boy's father faces the friend. The movements in the play keep shifting from one house to the other. In the first movement Rangannaraya while questioning the 1st Friend is told that Sripati has been mentally disturbed by some personal problems. The father enquires if he has some problems at college. The movement shifts to the house of Sarasu where her mother Amma is worried about her melancholic look and loss of appetite. Amma considers it as the consequence of karma of her past life when she lost her husband. Though Sarasu lacks nothing in life, she keeps crying. The mother wants to know the reasons for it. However, Sarasu explains it all away saying that she was dieting to be beautiful. She also tells her mother that she wouldn't marry. Since she had lost her only son, the mother insists that Sarasu has to fill the vacuum in the family giving her a grandson.

Rangannaraya tells the 1st Friend about his own struggle of life being from a lower middle class background. When his wife died after giving birth to Sripati, he raised the boy with the help of his sister Atte. Now he is ready for anything provided his son gets married. He enquires if Sripati has any girls in mind. The playwright employs the technique of juxtaposition of movements in both the houses.

In scene 2, four young men enter with Sripati and interact with each other. They discuss what Sripati himself had confessed that he would never accept dowry. On the other hand Mama and Amma discuss plans of marriage for Sarasu who is in love with Sripati. Both the parties are engaged in discussing on matching of horoscopes though Sripati never believed in such superstitions. Ironically the 2nd Friend comments, '... I always knew our forefathers were clever. They always said, 'Agnisakshi. Agni is my witness'!... But I guess such Shastras have to continue' (*SITD* 81). As the horoscopes of both Sripati and Sarasu match, the conversation in both the houses focus on dowry as Sripati used to give lecture on the topic being the president of Anti Dowry Sangha.

> **Atte** (*To Rangannaraya*) That's enough. Stop talking like an imbecile. (*to Amma*) Is it in our hands to refuse? Some families take it as a matter of honour to offer a dowry. How do we say no then?
>
> **Rangannaraya**: (*Appreciating his sister's intelligence*) That's true. Just as we have the right to refuse dowry, you have the freedom to offer us one.
>
> **Amma**: But if we give it against the boy's wishes, his principles, he may harass our daughter. That frightens us.
>
> **Mama**: (*To Rangannaraya*) ...What's so complicated about it! If you feel like giving dowry, make out a cheque in the name of Rangannaraya. That's all. Why should the boy know?...(85).

As Sripati's Friends express their premonition that he would refuse to accept any dowry, the family members agree that there would be no quarrelling over the issue. However, Atte states clearly that the girl's side has to give something for the marriage expenses and for the setting up of a new home.

In Scene 3 Rangannaraya and Mama are both deeply immersed in thought. From the discussion it is clear that the episode takes place six months after the wedding of Sripati and Sarasu. Amma complains about her solitary life after marriage. Atte insists that Rangannaraya lets Sarasu go to her mother's house. Amma is also of the same opinion until the couple finds a separate house of their own. Meanwhile Rangannaraya suggests that Sarasu takes up a small job in addition to Sripati who has a Ph.D. degree which is expected to fetch him a decent employment.

Act II opens with Sripati's bedroom. In anger he grabs Sarasu's hand and drags her in and questions her on the things brought into the house – cots, chairs, table etc..

> **Sarasu**: When you are not here, the door to the room is locked till five in the evening.
>
> **Sripati**: (*Surprised*) So where are you the whole day? Don't you come here occasionally at least? 'No,'
>
> *(she shakes her head*) What the hell is going on in this house?
>
> **Sarasu**: (*Pulls her hand away, and moves aside*) Nothing that concerns you...(*Starts to leave*)
>
> **Sripati**: (*Grabs her by the hand and stops her*) Wait! I'll call Atte. I'll ask her what's going on.
>
> **Sarasu**: (*Terrified now*) I beg of you, please don't. I should never have said anything to you, but now it's done. If she knows I have told you, my life... (*bites back her words and stops abruptly*)
>
> **Sripati** (*Disdainfully*) Why are you so scared? This house belongs to you...to me, not to her. (*Points to all the furniture*) I want to ask her where all this has come from? (98-99).

This episode reveals certain hidden fears Sarasu has when she says, 'If she knows I have told you, my life...' Sripati fails to take the cue from it.

When he questions Atte about the matter, she cooks up the story and accuses Sarasu of secretly getting the things from her family. The episode climaxes in Atte hitting Sarasu accusing her of having told lies to her husband. She further accuses Sripati being hand in gloves with his wife. Though Sarasu apologises to her, Atte keeps her grudge.

In the meantime Sripati's friends ironically speak of dowry. Sripati gets annoyed and reaffirms his determination to fight the malady, hearing of the case of a woman burned to death for dowry. Her is also told about the non-confidence motion against him as the president of the anti-Dowry Sangha, since he is accused of having accepted dowry himself.

When his father returns, Sripati demands that everything brought into the house be returned. Though Sripati is keen to live by his ideals, his father laments the financial crunch of the family struggling to get a loan to offer as bribe to get a job for his son. Atte suggests that Sarasu gets the loan from her mother. But Rangannaraya has premonitions that his son would resist the plan.

In Act III Atte and sarasu are seen conversing on the problems they face. Atte expresses her anger at the men – Rangannaraya is a helpless man and Sripati has no job of his own. Atte tries to cajole Sarasu and pretends to be intimate with her. Sarasu expresses her fear of being with Atte and tries to get out of the room. All of a sudden Atte becomes very threatening and she drags Sarasu and makes her lie down.

> **Atte**: Will you do as I say? Or else this room will be locked to you at night too, as it is in the day. If Sripati forces me, I'll tell him, 'I swear that if you sleep with your wife, it will be like sleeping with me.'...I'm a wretched widow, and now at my age I can say anything...Say you are sorry. (*Sarasu meekly does so*) Tomorrow you'll go to your mother. I have a mission for you. Fulfil it before returning (118-119).

There is total darkness on stage and the scene shifts to Atte screaming, 'Will someone please save my daughter-in-law?' (119). The audience gets an illusory feeling that the play ends here in the dark. But the siren of an ambulance is heard as the lights come on. Amma and Mama are on stage. Amma is agitated and wants to bring her daughter back home. She has premonition that they would kill her daughter.

Amma is scared of Atte the wretched widow as 'She is a witch who will destroy the happiness of a young couple, just because she never experienced that joy herself' (122).

The scene shifts to the room where Atte tells Sarasu to follow her direction to get Rs.15,000/- from her mother to offer as bribe to get a job for her husband. Sarasu replies saying that she would do it only with permission from Sripati. The altercation leads to the bride burning.

> **Atte**: Are you trying to cheat me, you bitch?
>
> **Sarasu**: Atte, aiyyo. Please don't pull out my hair...That...that's fire. Aiyyo....Fire, fire... Save me Atte! My sari! Aiyyo. I'm dying. I'm dying...(*Gradually Sarasu's cries die*) (123).

After sometime Atte comes out on to the stage sniffing her hand and throwing away the matches. She begins to beat her breasts and cry aloud, 'Aiyyo, aiyyo, my darling daughter-in-law. Someone, please come, save her. Aiyyo... her sari has caught fire. My daughter. Can anyone save her?' (123)

The scene shifts with the sound of siren of a passing ambulance coming and receding. Chatter of people can be heard commenting on the girl's death as a case of murder. A voice is heard demanding that the husband be thrown into the funeral pyre along with the corpse. The play ends as Amma and Mama walk across with faces covered, since Sarasu has become an 'Agnisakshi' with fire as the witness to her gruesome murder.

The play is a powerful examination of a social concern that plagues the Indian society with the ever increasing cases of bride burning.

3. Yama Vanquished

Yama Vanquished is a brief farce in one act where Yama the God of Death meets a sick man. The emaciated old man, sick in bed, is uncomfortable with the expression of perpetual worry. He groans and moans, calling his wife and others. He feels as though someone has come calling him.

> **Sick Man**: ...Aiyyo! Someone has come! He's beckoning me with his finger! An ugly dark man! Aiyyo! No, no, I am not going to die. Doctor, please do something for me!...No, no, I'm not ready to go yet!

Yama: (*With arrogance*) Hey, you low creature! Who will listen to you when you moan, 'No, no I don't want to die'? Your time is up. It's time to leave this world behind (126).

Yama tells the old man to be ready for reckoning. But he pleads with him to let him get a little better. Yama does not care about the excuses made by the sick man. The farcical arguments make the audience laugh hilariously, yet it conveys thought provoking ideas. Meanwhile the doctor comes to examine the sick man and tells him that he has nothing to worry about. The doctor tells him not to bother about Yama, considering him to be only a visiting lunatic medicine man from the mental asylum. But Yama retorts:

Yama: This man's time is up. That is why I, Yama, am here. Have you understood? And

you say there is no danger to his life!

...

Doctor: Then you have nothing to fear. He probably went crazy while studying Ayurveda.

...

Yama: (*Yells*)...Do you think you can protect him from fetters of death?...

... (*Irritated)* You arrogant, lowly creature, you still don't believe me? (131).

Soon the wife of the sick man arrives and begins to abuse Yama, boasting about her Brahmin origin. Yama ironically tells her that she is fortunate to have her husband freed from the bondage of Yama. Still she keeps abusing her husband and is ready to leave him.

However, the sick man gets out of his bed the moment he learns that his boss is about to visit him. He gets ready to welcome him and promises to invite Yama for the tea party. His wife is thrilled to see him out of bed and requests Yama to make frequent visits to the sick man.

Wife: If you want to set him right, this is the only way.

Yama: (*Looking at her with awe*) Amma, your devotion is truly great. You desire only the well-being of your husband. That is why I will spare his life.

Wife: Whoever you are, you have been lucky for me. At least he has gone back to work and left me in peace. Why don't you come here every day? (136).

The comedy brings to focus realities of life. Though Yama's beckoning is inevitable, the fear of death can make man come to terms with life. Unlike in *Everyman*, here it is Yama that brings the sick man to live a better life.

4. Ramarajya

Ramarajya is a political satire. The playwright exposes that in politics only names keep changing while the spirit of the game remains the same at all times. Scene I is set in the main street in the capital where a huge crowd is on the move. Hayavadana and Krishtu are part of the crowd pushing around to gather the news of the announcement of the names of ministers. They strike up a conversation with others in the crowd regarding the rumours of who the Prime Minister would be. Meanwhile someone shouts, 'Ravana is dead.' 'Victory to Rama.' (138)

The conversation now centres on how Rama has won his kingdom and it is going to be Rama's Rajya. But it is rumoured that Rama had not agreed to it. Rama didn't want to rule all by himself, instead he preferred it to be done by his ministers without a king. As someone commented: 'What can I say? You can surely figure it out yourselves. Didn't Bharata rule the kingdom in the name of Rama? So if he could rule all in the name of just one person why shouldn't one person Rama rule in the name of one and all? This is Rama's idea' (139).

It was rumoured that all may be made ministers when the list would be published in the Rama Rajya. Rama might give up his power and abdicate his throne, but not his right to rule. Who would be his successor? The chatter of people continue and the rumour is spread that Sita or Kaikeyi would be Deputy Prime Minister. Ministerial positions may be given to Bharata, Lakshmana and even Hanuman since the monkeys are agile in leaping on to ministers' seats.

Scene II is set in a large hall in the palace where Rama is seated at the head of the table facing the spectators. With him are Sita, Lakshmana, Shatrughna, Bharata, Kaikeyi, Sugriva, Vibhishana and Maricha. Rama addresses everyone and expresses gratitude for having shared his responsibility for fourteen years of his exile. He begins to pay homage to his deceased father and king Dasharatha.

Rama further declares that in his Rajya all citizens would be free and equal. Maricha suggests that since the idea originated from Rama, it could be called Ramarajya. Rama promises that as long as unity exists among them, it would be an ideal nation. He also thought of increasing ministerial posts instead of reducing them to ensure the welfare of citizens.

Soon a citizen brought in by Bharata, challenges Rama for having appointed Sita his Deputy Prime Minister. Instantly Sita vacates her seat as a sign of resigning her post. When others object to such an injustice, Rama replies, '...Don't you know the first principle of Ramarajya is to accept your own mistake?' (149).

Sriranga's technique is story telling through his plays giving them farcical element and basing them on popular or folk culture. He employs folktale and mythic patterns and yet making them relevant to modern man. His message is at the same time serious in nature. Theatre is meant to communicate to the audience dialogues, gestures and movements, making it a social ritual. As Mahesh Dattani would opine, 'A play text could be staged. The creative process involved was to take the page to the stage' (Dattani 38). Sriranga has been very successful in presenting theatre and life through his plays- analysing social life.

References

Banker, B.K. "Indian Theatre, Yesterday and Today: An Overview." *The Journal of Indian Writing in English*. Vol.24. July. No.2, 1996.

Dattani, Mahesh. *Indian Literature: Sahitya Akademi's Bi-monthly Journal*. July-August. Vol.XLIX. No.4. 2005.

Esslin, Martin. *The Theatre of the Absurd*. London: Penguin, 1968.

—— "The Absurd Movement in Kannada Theatre: An Overview." *New Quest*. November-December, 1996.

Mukherjee, Tutun. *Girish Karnad's Plays: Performance and Critical Perspectives*. Delhi: Pencraft International, 2006.

Reddy, K. Venkata, R.K. Dhawan. *Flowering of Indian Drama: Growth and development*. New Delhi: Prestige Books, 2004.

Reddy, P. Obula. "Cultural Heterogeneity in Indian Drama." *Flowering of Indian Drama: Growth and Development.* New Delhi: Prestige Books, 2004.

Sebastian, A.J, Chandra, N.D.R. *Literary Terms in Drama, Theatre & Cinema.* Delhi: Authorspress, 2002.

Shivarudrappa, G.S. *Indian Literature: Sahitya Akademi's Bi-monthly Journal.* Sept-Oct. Vol.XLIII. No.5. 1999.

Sriranga. *Shadows in the Dark: Four Plays by Sriranga.* Trans. Usha Desai. Bangalore : Unisun Publications, 2007. (Abbreviated : *SITD*).

10

Appearance and Reality in Girish Karnad's *Wedding Album*

1. Introduction

The plays of Girish Karnard (1938-) have been universal in appeal with "efficacy and entertainment... to urge a socio-cultural interrogation" (Mukherjee 22). In his *Wedding Album*, the story moves like a collage of snapshots exploring appearance and reality in the midst of socio-cultural and familial relationships. It gives insights into contemporary middle-class Indian society in the wake of technological advancement. The play is humorous and comical, marked by irony, multiple issues and questions of social and emotional nature. It progresses like the modern day TV serials, presenting a realistic family situation. It also demystifies middle class South Indian Brahmin marriage (Srinivasan x) in the backdrop of familial and emotional relationships, their choices, values and life styles. An Indian wedding is an occasion for a family to bring together all the relatives and friends to show their solidarity and family ties. In the process the family also has to cope up with anxieties concerning dowry and other financial burdens while maintaining its social status.

Karnad presents the story surrounding Vidula Nadkarni's wedding in the form of a television serial. One of the characters in the play, Pratibha, a producer of television programmes, however find the plot not sufficiently appropriate for an episode saying, "How can you make a character interesting in a tele-serial when you are not interested in her in real life?" (*WA* 9). As the play progresses, each scene reveals some hidden secrets of human yearning as the characters continue in their search for emotional and sexual fulfilment. The older members find it difficult to adjust to modern lifestyles in the technologically advanced world. The new generation on the other hand has its own ambitious plans of easy success. They have their dreams to scale and seek emotional fulfilment in sexual freedom, ignoring certain values and traditions.

2. Progress in the play

The playwright lets scenes one and five take place about three years after the episodes in the play, to suit his application of the tele-serial technique. Scene one opens with the central character Vidula, a self conscious girl, speaking in front of a camera. She makes her attempt to introduce herself, her background and interests as her brother Rohit is making a video film on her, to be mailed to a prospective gentleman caller from America. Rohit is offscreen, directing her to show her best to be attractive. She is tired of the several reshootings. As she speaks in front of the camera, all information about her and the family is listed one by one:

- She is a twenty two years old Geography graduate willing to go to USA after her marriage.
- Her father Dr. Nadkarni is a retired government doctor.
- She has an elder sister Hema who is married and lives in Australia.
- Rohit, her elder brother, is engaged in writing script for TV production of teleplays.
- She discloses a guarded family secret about a mentally retarded brother who had died in childhood. Humorously she also adds that she is not retarded, but possesses high CQ (Cooking Quotient).

The scene continues with the editing of the film in a Software Production Office by Pratibha and Rohit. Pratibha dumps Vidula's story incredible though Rohit tells her it happened three years ago. The argument continues:

> PRATIBHA: ...They may believe it, but they won't like it. A girl from an educated middle-
> class family – a graduate – agrees to consider marrying a man whom she has
> never met....in this day and age?
> ROHIT: They were not total strangers. I mean, they had exchanged video tapes. SMSed.
> Talked on the phone. And he belonged to our caste (8).

Rohit continues to give more details about his sister who was a very decent and innocent girl who never had any relationships with boys. She was married off to the boy from USA, after exchanging video tapes and spending a few days together in a hotel. But Pratibha being bored with the story, switches over to episode ten about the cook Radhabai and her mad daughter.

As the episode is being edited, the conversation focuses on Rohit's own life - how he got married under familial pressures to Tapasya, a girl not of his choice, after he had gone steady with Isabel, a Christian girl. His pregnant wife had gone to Hyderabad to visit her parents. In the meantime, Isabel had joined Pratibha's company. She had confided to Pratibha how she was emotionally broken after Rohit broke up with her. Both of them had their own stories to narrate. Isabel thought he broke off when Tapasya's father financed his trip to Germany. On his part Rohit blamed Isabel breaking off when they were about to be engaged. Now, Pratibha questions why he had invited Isabel to dinner when his wife was away: "On the day your wife left for Hyderabad! You didn't mention that you were alone at home. But she guessed. She knows you well... Since then you have asked her again. Twice within ten days. In spite of her refusal" (61). Pratibha continues to daunt Rohit with her own marriage to a Muslim who she married three years ago when anti-Muslim riots surged only because he offered her affection and security. When she invites him along with Tapasya for dinner, Rohit utters "bitch" indicating his exposed guilt.

3. Appearance and reality in the various episodes

Scene two takes place in the living room of Nadkarni's home. Vidula, Hema and their mother are engaged in selecting silk sarees to be given to various relatives on the occasion of the wedding. The mother is very conscious of keeping the purchases affordable. The cook Radhabai comes in to add to the comical element in the play. The father is seated on a chair with newspaper in hand. But obviously he is not concentrated in reading as he puts it down occasionally looking at the horizon. He is bored with life as he yawns and keeps uttering "I am so bored or time just won't move" (10). He wished if his late brother Ramdas were around to help.

The mother had planned to purchase a necklace for Hema, who on the contrary, expressed her desire not to waste any money on her. The mother was keen to gift it to her as her marriage was arranged all of a sudden fifteen years ago, when they were not in a position to buy her any gold. Hema's mother begged her father to arrange some gold for her, but he didn't make fuss over it since his son-in-law didn't ask for anything.

Joining the conversation, the father began to recount the reality of how he grew up in poverty along with his brother Ramdas. They had to share a plate of gruel and went from relative to relative for survival. They received education through scholarship from Saraswat Education Society.

As the mother goes to the kitchen, Hema and Vidula strike up their conversation on their lives. The con a typical Indian middle class way of putting up appearances even among family members. Hence, Hema speaks of her husband's successful life as a banker. The Indians like him run the whole commercial world in America. Being transferred from place to place, Indian boys prefer to marry Indian girls who will trail after their husbands' footsteps like obedient Sati Savitris. Hema also considers her life similar to that of her mother, even though her husband has a top job.

The conversation is interrupted by Vivan the boy next door, who comes to return borrowed books. As Vidula busies herself on the phone, he tells Hema that he had a letter for her in the book. Reading it she was shocked by its content. Immediately he kept another more pungent letter on the sofa. Vidula happens to read the content: "Darling, you don't know how I desire to crush you in my arms" (19). As Hema snatched away the letter, Vidula thinks the love letter came from Hema's husband. The episode reveals moral degradation of even youngsters in a society that boasts of its integrity.

The episode moves on to mother and the cook Radhabhai quarrelling in the kitchen. The scene is a revelation of the reality of the poor being sexually exploited. Radhabai keeps complaining that she had no choice but continue to live in their home after the death of her husband. She threatens to leave as she often did, but finally refuses to move out as she has nowhere to go. The story reveals how Radhabai was married and had a daughter Yamuna. Since they were so poor Yamuna came to Bangalore and got a job and sent money home. When her husband died, Radhabai came to Bangalore and worked as cook in a family. The following day a messenger came to take her to where her daughter lived. To her utter shock, she found Yamuna living as a concubine of a trader. Radhabai left to continue her job as a cook and never mentioned about her daughter to anyone. After a couple of years, she lost all communication with Yamuna and found that she was abandoned by the trader. She saw Yamuna in the street, gone mad and searching for her mother. That was the last time she saw her daughter.

The reality of middle class weddings in our social set up is like a gamble as shown in the following sequence. Rohit comes to inform that Ashwin would arrive only a few days later and he would meet Vidula and spend time with her. If they liked each other then they would go ahead with the wedding, otherwise they would part as friends. The mother was very upset over his delayed coming and wanted to break off the engagement. Ashwin and Vidula had seen each other on tapes. He had said he didn't want any fuss over a wedding with rituals. Others in the family were unhappy with such arrangements, but Rohit found Vidula and Ashwin satisfied with their electronic friendship through tape and mobile. The father was ready for anything as he considered marriage a gamble. He only wished his brother Ramdas were there to do the needful.

Rohit shows his annoyance with Vidula for spending several hours daily at the internet parlour playing video games instead of applying for her birth certificate required for getting her passport. When Hema enquired what she did at the café, Vidula merely said she listened to sermons by Swami Ananga Nath.

Scene three brings in the conversation between father and Rohit in the company of family friends Gopal Hattangadi Vatsala Hattangadi, Mohan Sirur and Mira Sirur. They recollect the earlier times when Ramdas was there to arrange everything for the wedding of Hema. The Hattangadi's have brought their daughter Tapasya along with the plan of fixing the nuptials between her and Rohit. Mohan and Mira are also with them to persuade Rohit to agree to the proposal. But Rohit shows his exasperation at their persisting in their proposal every week when they called on them as he had been dating Isabel, a Christian girl. They even try to bribe him with the plan of sending him abroad. Rohit gets bothered and keeps saying he was not interested in the marriage. The bargain continues among them for a long time, but Rohit remains firm in his noncommittal attitude. Gopal shows his helplessness and pleads pathetically, "...we have told everyone in Hyderabad that this alliance has been finalized. Everyone there thinks we are here for the engagement ceremony... Her classmates have actually thrown a party to celebrate the event... She is our only child, Rohit. She is sensitive. Don't hurt her, please, don't wound her... I'll fall to your feet..." (39). Gopal nearly breaks down and kneels to touch Rohit's feet while he recoils in horror. As Rohit excuses himself to go in a hurry, Mohan requests him to reconsider his stand. As they leave Rohit gets Isabel's call and tells her of the ordeal he had been through with the Sirurs. He expresses his inability to be with her. Overhearing the conversation, Hema shows her botheration in his not dating a girl from their own community. Vidula reprimands him for not having been firm with the party in saying about his relationship with Isabel. She teases him how he wields power over them: "To have a girl waiting for you – her parents kneeling before you – begging and pleading... It really must make you feel grand" (42).

Scene four begins with Hema returning home and finding Vivan browsing through books. She tells him to leave as the family is to have an important meeting. She scolds him who is younger than her son, for writing filthy love letters to her. He speaks out his heart telling her that he fell desperately in love with her and longs to die kissing her. He is convinced of his infatuation for her and hands over two letters which she puts into her handbag.

The family gathers to discuss the mistaken entry in Vidula's birth certificate where her uncle Ramdas's name was entered as father. The mother is convinced that it was no mistake, but done deliberately by Ramdas to blacken their face. She begs them not to reveal it to their father lest he might die of shame.

In scene six Vidula visits the internet café and begins her chat with her secret lover who had been pining for her being addicted to her. She tells him she is being sold off in marriage. The conversation reveals her ironic view of marriage.

> VIDULA: I have been sold off...I told you I am a kept woman. Kept by a trader. I am his concubine. Maintained by a man much older than me... He is dying. He has had a heart attack. Last

night. He is in the ICU. Could be dead by tomorrow. His family is bound to throw me out. So I had to find a new master. A young man. He lives in the US. He has paid a good price to my family.

VOICE: Tell me your name and address and I'll come and buy you.

VIDULA: Thanks, mate. I knew you would say that. You are nice (64-5).

The matter stated by Vidula is from her subconscious with reference to the fate of Radhabai's daughter who was kept by a trader. It also refers to her father who they feared would get an attack if he knew of the game played by Ramdas claiming to be the father of Vidula in the birth certificate. She continues to indulge in internet sex with the secret lover. But she gets scary of the rest of the intimate movements as the Hindu vigilante youth make commotion outside. The Hindu youth charges Vidula for indulging in porno films. As one of them threatens her with dire consequences, the second youth attempts to calm him down and let her go since she belonged to his caste. When she is warned never to return, Vidula challenges them and accuses them for having molested her and attempted to rape. She demands that police be called in. The scene mocks at the fundamentalists trying to extort money in the name of maintaining cultural tradition and moral values. The attendant reveals how the youth keep coming to the café whenever they fall short of money.

This scene is suggestive of the sex porn to which young people get so easily addicted. Individual's hidden inner sexual cravings are exposed by the dramatist, revealing certain aberrations in society and those who take law into their own hands in the name of moral disciplining.

Scene seven brings to focus father and mother expecting Ashwin, the boy from America. The mother wonders how Vidula who is timid will cope up meeting for the first time a total stranger. The fathers' comment "parents are irrelevant to their growing up" (73) presents the irony of the hidden truth of the matter. They never could imagine, Vidula whom they took to be a shy and inexperienced girl, had been indulging in secret internet sex. chat.

The scene shifts to the father searching for the wedding accounts of Hema which his brother Ramdas had kept. He is full of praises for him. But his wife shows her annoyance the way he still regarded Ramdas faithful although he hated her husband and had done him wrong. The father accepts facts and sympathises with him instead, for having been a failure all his life. The conversation also draws attention to disruption of their family life with the father's frequent transfers from place to place, making children grow up with aunts and relatives.

In scene eight Ashwin and Vidula are in serious conversation with each other. Ashwin confesses he is passing through a spiritual crisis. His only condition for marriage is that she shares his spiritual quest. He speaks of his successful career having everything he longed for, including girl friends and mistresses. Now he has reached the fag end coming to the conclusion "that whole culture is empty of values now, bereft of any living meaning...The European Industrial revolution began by rejecting religion in favour of material values. But today the legacy is strangling the West. They have no spiritual moorings left. They are adrift in a godless, amoral world" (80). He has come looking for a life partner who carries within her the essence of Hindu spirituality, innocence and purity. "Someone like you carries within youth essence of Hindu spirituality. Woman as Mother, Wife, Daughter. Womanhood as the most sacred ideal.... I want you to see this not merely as a marriage but as a mission. I would like you to be my partner in carrying the best of our spiritual tradition to the west and save the West" (81-2).The irony is that the partner he finds in Vidula is a girl far from his idealistic expectations – a girl who indulges in sexual fantasies and perversions in secret in the midst of the vigilante youth who attempt to perpetrate fake religious fervour. His expectations are too idealistic like St. John in Charlotte Bronte's *Jane Eyre,* who wishes to marry Jane to be his wife and helpmate in an idealistic mission. "God and nature intended you for a missionary's wife. It is not personal, but mental endowments they have given you: you are formed for labour, not for love....You shall be mine: I claim you – not for my pleasure, but for my Sovereign's service" (Bronte 424). Ashwin like St. John has fallen in love with a mission and not with a person. Such idealism in spousal relationship will only wreck it as the type of love remains purely in the level of empty love.

Though scene nine is one of parting of characters, it reveals how Vidula had spent eight days with Ashwin in the hotel to know each others before deciding on their commitment in marriage. She agreed to fall in line with his demands. In the course of the conversation, Hema tells Vidula that she shouldn't hesitate to divorce him if the marriage does not get on well in America. Rohit seconds the opinion as divorce is considered a common thing in modern times. But strangely Vidula has taken to live by Ashwin's principles becoming a vegetarian and deciding never to divorce him.

As they leave the father makes his comment on marriage as a gamble which none can escape. The mother on her part taking Vidula aside gives her parting advice that she shouldn't miss opportunities she may get in America to explore her talents. The mother bemoans her lost dreams becoming a mother at an early age, so too Hema becoming merely a housewife. She challenges Vidula to make use of the opportunities in the modern world. The father adds his final comments on how the mother had made all the difference in the family sacrificing herself for the sake of everyone. "If we are all happily gathered together here, if we have been a such a loving family, the credit must go to your mother" (91). The play is an excellent portrayal of a modern day wedding in contrast to traditional Indian marital relationship.

4. Appearance and reality in interpersonal relationships

The characters in their interpersonal relationship can be analysed applying the triangular theory of love propounded by psychologist Robert Sternberg. He examines love from three components:intimacy, passion, and decision/commitment. These may operate in combination or separately from one another. Accordingly, love can be classified into seven distinct kinds as shown below. The different kinds of love lets individuals to understand and communicate the types of emotional behaviours they express. Consummate love is the ideal and complete love, combining intimacy, passion and commitment (Sternberg).

Different types of love can be classified either individually or in combination of these components. A particular type of love in course of time can be transformed into another type.

Various types of love among the characters:

TYPES OF LOVE	INTIMACY	PASSION	COMMITMENT	CHARACTERS IN RELATIONSHIP
Nonlove				
Liking/friendship	X			
Infatuated love		X		i. Vidula's relationship with internet lover ii. Vivan's relationship with Hema
Empty love			X	i. Rohit's relationship with Tapasya ii. Ramdas's relationship with Dr. Nadkarni
Romantic love	X	X		i. Rohit's relationship with Isabel
Companionate love	X		X	i. Relationships in Dr. Nadkarni's household ii. Relationship between Vidula and Ashwin iii. Dr. Nadkarni's relationship with Ramdas
Fatuous love		X	X	i. Ramdas' relationship with Mrs. Nadkarni
Consummate love	X	X	X	i. Relationship between Dr. Nadkarni and wife ii. Relationship between Hema and husband iii. Relationship between Pratibha and husband iv. Isabel's relationship with Rohit

- **Nonlove** is the absence of all three components of love.
- **Liking/friendship** is intimate love in which a person feels a bondedness with another. There is no intense passion or commitment.
- **Infatuated love** is pure passion. Romantic relationships often begin as infatuated love and leads to romantic love as intimacy develops in course of time. Infatuated love may disappear all of a sudden if it does not develop intimacy or commitment.
- **Empty love** is characterized by commitment without intimacy or passion. In the case of most arranged marriages, relationships often begin as empty love, but in course of time may develop into one of the other forms.
- **Romantic love** hinges on intimacy and passion, thereby bonding individuals emotionally and physically through passionate arousal.
- **Companionate love** is intimate and non-passionate type of love. It has the element of long-term commitment devoid of sexual desire. Such love is found in marriages in which passion has gone

out of the relationship leading to deep affection and commitment. The ideal love relationship among family members is a kind of companionate love. Such relationship between close friends lead to platonic love.

- **Fatuous love** is characterised by sudden courtship and marriage through passion and commitment. It lacks stable intimacy and partners share passionate or sexual moments only out of commitment. It tends more to Empty love.
- **Consummate love** is the fullness of agape love which is an ideal relationship between a perfect couple. However such an ideal love can deteriorate into companionate love when passion declines (Ibidem).

5. Conclusion

In *Wedding Album* Karnad has been very innovative in depicting appearance and reality. He handles deftly absurd situations and strange sequences in a passing manner, raising too many passing questions and issues that plague contemporary Indian society. Behind every such passing issue there is a deep rooted mystery the playwright subtly presents such as: Ramdas making false entry regarding the fatherhood of Vidula; his attempts to be close to his sister-in-law and being her protector when her husband used to abuse her. The mystery remains – was there an illicit relationship between Ramdas and Vidula's mother? Is Ramdas Vidula's biological father? In passing Karnard makes his readers and audience pay attention several issues that plague modern Indian society. The sequence where Vidula consents to marry, coming to terms with Ashwin's ideological dreams, sounds very unrealistic. Vidula, though appears to be a traditional girl, is far from it in her behaviour and life style. Her suppressed sexual fulfilment in the internet café and Hema's response to the young Vivan are hidden problems afflicting our society. Karnad's introducing the sequence of Radhabai's mad daughter, though superadded, exposes rampant sexual pervasion and abuse in society. The play may be assessed as a superb commentary on appearance and reality in a society that is caught up in the backdrop of globalization and technological progress. The story is deplete with abrupt situations and episodes like in an absurd drama. Though hilarious, the story exposes suppressed frustrations and sexual games people play under cover of maintaining traditional values.

Works Cited:

Bronte, Charlotte. *Jane Eyre*. Oxford: Oxford University Press, re-set 1993.

Karnad, Girish. *Wedding Album*. New Delhi: Oxford University Press, 2009. Abbreviated: *WA*.

Mukherjee, Tutun. "Introduction." *Girish Karnad's Plays: Performance and Critical Perspectives*. Delhi: Pencraft International, 2006.

Srinivasan, Amrit. "Foreword." Girish Karnad. *Wedding Album*. New Delhi: Oxford University Press, 2009.

Sternberg, Robert. "Triangular theory of love" http://en.wikipedia.org/wiki/Triangular theory_of_love. Downloaded on 16 July 2009.

11

Badal Sircar's *Life of Bagala*: A study in human will and determination

Badal Sircar (1925 -), the Bengali dramatist, is known as the innovator of contemporary Indian theatre. with his oeuvre of nearly fifty plays. Though a trained civil engineer and town planner, he took a keen interest in theatre. Dismayed by the paucity of Bengali drama, he began writing plays from 1950s. With his flair for comedy he wrote witty plays in the everyday speech of middle-class people of Culcutta. He is concerned with the pointlessness of existence, compounded by a sense of associative guilt and responsibility in disturbed persons belonging to the urban middle class, in a world of increasing violence and inhumanity. As a producer, he conceptualized *anganmancha* or Third Theatre, which abandoned proscenium stages and performed in a bare room or open space with spectators sitting all around. Though he had his conventional theatre group *Satabdi* (Century) since 1967, Sircar opted for the Third Theatre which broke the barriers between performer and spectator, performer and performer, spectator and spectator. He wanted theatre to be a collective exercise to awaken and enhance the social consciousness of people. In the process he achieved the involvement of villagers with whom he lived during the process of some plays in writing and production ("Badal Sircar"http://www.indianetzone.com).

During the course of his engineering assignments in India and abroad, he kept up his playwriting with the purpose of social transformation. Though he subscribed to a leftist worldview earlier, eventually, he lost his faith in the official left position(*TP* xiv).

Sircar found naturalistic theatre which sought to depict life as it is, by creating separation between audience and actors, not a dramatic form of his taste. He wanted to break the barrier and create easy communication between the actors and the audience. He stuck to the open-air-format with the purpose of creating awareness among people about socio-economic oppression (xxiii). The Third Theatre is flexible, portable and inexpensive without having to depend on props, costumes and other paraphernalia of naturalistic theatre (*TP* xxiv). It has been the result of Sircar's attempt at creating a theatre of synthesis by trying to break through the system of 'story' and 'characters' to give prominence to 'theme' and 'types.' His method was one of addressing directly to the spectators than mere 'dialogue' between stage characters, through physical 'acting' than 'language' (Lal 427). Thus he has been very effective through his plays to spread his ideas.

Life of Bagala (Bagalacharitmanas) opens with two Stage Managers standing together to blow their imaginary trumpets. They repeat the imaginary action but no hero enters. They keep shouting "Ente-r the hero! Hero! Hero! Ente-r the hero!" (53). They search for the hero in the audience. Suddenly a simple ordinary person comes out from the crowd, showing his disgust with life. As the trumpets keep blowing, the hero keeps covering his ears though he neither sees nor hears them. He utters his helplessness: "Seems I'm losing my mind. All of a sudden… as if someone's blowing a trumpet. But I was to blow the trumpet. Since childhood…" (54). The Stage managers introduce the hero, Bagalacharan Batabyal. He utters that he should have been thrown into the Ganges with a 10 kg stone tied to his neck since orphaned from childhood, when his parents died in a bus mishap. He curses his unfortunate lot since he is ill-treated by his guardians.

Baga then returns to his childhood when he used to be taunted by his school friends. The Stage Managers join making fun of him, pulling his hair. As the dancing goes on, his college days are recalled with a Professor taking attendance. While all students pronounce their names, Bagala is reluctant to do so. When he utters his name 'Batabyal,' all make fun of him calling 'Batball.' As the Professor further asks questions on his identity, it is revealed, how after the untimely death of his parents, he was looked after by his maternal uncle.

As his friends poke fun at him, his aunt arrives to chide him for forgetting to buy fish at the end of the day from the fishmonger. Bagala tells her that the fishmonger refused to sell him fish with scales taken out as she instructed him.

BAGALA: No aunt. It 's true. He said... taking off scales for fishweighing 250 grams.

...

AUNT: 250 grams! Shall I buy 1 kg fish and feed you? How much money did your daddy
leave behind? (59).

When the aunt leaves in a rage, his uncle comes in asking for the batteries he had told him to purchase. He excuses himself for not purchasing it as he had to go far away to Sambhuda's shop. Bagala asks his uncle to buy a bicycle for him to do errands. Meanwhile, the aunt tells him to coach Mantu, her son in maths.

A group of boys and girls enter and dance around clapping hands. The Stage Managers separate themselves and announce that Bagala, the hero, is at his maternal uncle's home. On his part he says humorously that there is no one to bash him up as he had received all the bashing in childhood.

The Stage Managers make their comments on how he burnt midnight oil to pass B.Com with flying colours. Though he attended several interviews, he never got a job. The sequence shifts to three interviewers questioning Bangala with irony and humour. Stammering, he is unable to respond to their questions. The sequence shifts to his uncle taunting him to get a job: "Somehow you'd grab a job...you'd be independent... though you've got nothing in these six months..." (61).

His aunt enters, admonishing him to put on some decent dress since they are to go to his would be father-in-law. But on his part, he refuses to marry. Their intention is to grab the fifty thousand rupees that is offered as dowry. He tells them that he would pay back all that they had invested in his studies, when he gets his salary from the job he would get. Telling him to put on his *dhoti-kurta*, his aunt tells him to be ready for the trip. He dances around fretting wildly with clenched teeth and uttering many meaningless words. The Stage Managers make their comment on the boy's behaviour:

STAGE MANAGER 1: This needs explanation. It is not *hysteria*. Our hero often resorts to
manifesting his anger and suppressed wrath in this manner.

STAGE MANAGER 2: In solitude and in subdued voice. Because he could never attain a
personality to speak his mind clearly in someone else's presence.
STAGE MANAGER 1: He has always preferred stepping back and escaping to plain
speaking in others' presence.

Fretting, Bagala continues to dance around wildly. He plans to run away with all he has in his pocket. He drops coin by coin on the floor: " Three rupees seventy-five paise. Oh! Done shopping over the years. Had I put away some money! I'd been *honest*! What've I got out of *honesty*? Three rupees seventy-five paise! *Honesty*? Nonsense! I was afraid to steal. Afraid. Simply afraid! Afraid of Uncle, afraid of Aunt, afraid of Mantu, afraid of the class-mates, afraid of the teachers, afraid of the Professor-s" (62-3).

Bagala continues to speak of his fear ingrained in him, of all sorts of people such as the neighbourhood boys, the clerk at the college office, the guard at the college gate, traffic police, grocers, bus conductors, peons, cows, dogs, lizards, cockroaches and spiders.

The Stage Managers continue to make comments about his honesty. He had been a servant without wages and a private tutor to Mantu. He is to marry an ugly, quarrelsome and pampered only daughter of an executive officer of a business house. The big dowry would go to the pockets of his uncle and aunt. Bagala has no courage to oppose their orders. If he marries and stays with his father-in-law, he would be given a job. The only option left for him is to disappear. But he is afraid of his uncle sending the police after him to get hold of the Rs.50000/- dowry. The Stage Managers get frustrated and leave while Bagala tells his aunt that his dhoti has been taken away by big rats.

The uncle searches for the missing Bagala and bargains with the neighbourhood boys, offering them five hundred rupees, instead of involving the police. As the uncle moves out, the boys laugh, sing and dance. The Stage Managers enter and blow trumpet to announce that Bagala has run away. The sequence moves to the sound of approaching train and Bagala going towards the railway tracks to commit suicide. Instantly an old man appears, talking to someone invisible. He talks all absurd things and about corruption in society:

> Listen. I'm a man. And men must die... Have to part with you if I die...Again sobbing?... We've been together for so long. Bound to feel bad. But when I die, you must fall in some able hands – got to settle it while I'm still alive...The country's full of thieves, swindlers, goons, frauds, black marketers and politicians – if you come into their hands, can you imagine what'll happen to the country? I was thinking of an honest person... Someone honest and decent yet poverty-stricken or in some difficulties (73).

Bagala enters and walks on the rail tracks and puts his head down to end his life. The old man observes him and tells the invisible person to pick him up from the tracks. A chorus enters in the form of a train. The invisible hand pulls him away and holds his wrist as the old man comes forward. The old man questions why Bagala attempted suicide. He wanted to know who had pulled him out of the tracks. The old man tells him it was Nila who saved him. He reveals to the old man why he opted to end his life, "My entire life...uncle, aunt, father-in-law, mother-in-law...Why'd I marry? I'd not marry" (74). The old man tells him that he suffers from nervous shock. He forces Bagala to move along with him on the tracks, though he resists. Bagala is curious to know who Nila is. The old man tells Nila could be any one - daughter, granddaughter or even mother.

The old man takes Bagala to his living room. To his utter surprise, Bagala finds dal, rice and fried pomfret fish served hot at that late night. The old man acknowledges that Nila has done all that so efficiently. When the boy regrets that he has not seen her, the old man signals him and communicates with someone invisible. Talking with the boy the old man learns that he has no bad habits such as smoking, boozing or stealing. He tells Bagala: "In short, you're extremely honest. And you- what I think – suffer from an inferiority complex. Moreover, you're too reticent. You got a first-class degree in B. Com, yet couldn't answer simple questions at the interview. Rather than facing life, you prefer escaping to a hole" (78).

Bagala lowers his face feeling ashamed of his position and the old man tells him that he utterly needs Nila to transform him. "You're her able inheritor. That's why I leave Nila in your hands... I'm not trying to marry off Nila with you. Actually, it's not even possible. Because Nila isn't a human being" (78). Offering a lighter, the old man makes him strike it to ignite the lamp. When he succeeds in striking the lighter after several attempts, he beholds a beautifully dressed gracious lady in blue in a dance-like movement, sitting on her knees. As he jumps up in shock, Nila begs him, her master, to order her. The old man introduces her as Nilpari whom he can see and listen to and give orders. He tells him that he can order her for whatever he wishes. When Bagala is totally confused, the old man tells him that it would take a bit of time to get used to her. On his part, Bagala makes gestures to indicate that he wishes her to disappear. The old man tells him to strike the lighter. Since Bagala is unable to strike the lighter, the old man demonstrates. When Bagala succeeds, Nila disappears. A frustrated old man tells him, "You can't be let alone with this at the moment. An extended *training* is required. You stay here for some time. Learn – how to summon Nila, give orders, and send her back" (81).

When Bagala stammers with fear, he is told that Nila would cook food and do all household chores. The old man tells him that he could stay with him in the small place and sleep. He reprimands Bagala for attempting to commit suicide since he didn't want to marry and stay at his father-in-law's. When he tells the old man about a job for him, he is told not to worry but to call Nila to make his bed to have a goodnight's rest. When he shows his reluctance to call Nila, the old man tells him that it is pure magic and the lamp is like that of Aladdin's magic lamp.

The Stage Managers comment on the hero who slept well on a bed brought by Nila till late afternoon the following day. When Bagala expresses his need to get a job, offering the lighter the old man tells him to call Nila. He is told to make a habit of calling Nila whenever he needs anything, considering her to be his girlfriend. The old man tells him to strike the lighter, but he is scared. The old man sums up the meaningless life Bagala lived: "Never ordered anyone in your life. Never made a request as well? Only followed what others ordered. That's why you were to marry and stay at father-in-law's following your uncle and aunt's order" (84). When he picks up courage and strikes the lighter, Nila appears and sits in front of him asking for his bidding. He orders her to get three most popular newspapers of the previous Sunday. He reads classified ad-s. Being unhappy with all the ad-s, he refers to an interview letter left at his uncle's home. The old man tells him to give the address to Nila to go and fetch it. The old man gives him practice for the interview and instils confidence in him. He is given a trial to speak out with courage at the interview. The old man reprimands him when he shows diffidence by looking elsewhere when questioned. Nila also prompts him how to speak properly. The mock interview, however, lets Bagala go out with a drooping head. The old man calls him back and Nila keeps her gaze on him. The old man warns him that he would never get a job and suggests that Nila could get him all he longs for. "You can hide in a room and live your life comfortably without an employment. Do you want it that way?" (91). The old man wants to know why he doesn't want to marry and stay at the father-in-law's. He warns him that unless he wards of his baseless fear, he would never get a job.

As the old man paces up and down, Nila shows her sympathy for Bagala and places her hand on his shoulders. Though surprised, he does not move away from her, but lowers his face after looking at her for a moment. Bagala strikes the lighter and Nila disappears.

The Stage Manager announces that the audience is able to see and listen to Nila for the sake of the play to continue. The old man strikes the lighter and Nila appears kneeling in front of him. As he talks to Nila he tells Bagala to go outside. But Nila tells him not to let Bagala go out, lest he would go towards the railway tracks to commit suicide. Nila reveal the main problem disturbing Bagala due to his uncle and aunt. "Their rough treatment and orders since childhood. Besides, all poking fun – as a result he got highly, what do they say – sensitive, about his name" (93). When the old man queries about possible therapy, Nila suggests that he should be kept alive to face his uncle and aunt.

The old man strikes the lighter and asks for Rs.10,100/-. Instantly a bag comes flying in and Nila disappears to Bagala's utter surprise. The old man tells him to go home and tell his uncle and aunt that he won't live there. If he can't face them, he could write a letter writing down all the expenses they had incurred for his food, clothing and studies and also returns in compensation Rs. 10,000/-. He is also given a hundred rupees for travel and other expenses. Striking the lighter he asks Nila from where the money came. She reveals it to be real money wasted in accidents. He doesn't pick up courage to write the letter and expresses reluctance to go to the house. Nila tells him to take her along with him to get courage. But he keeps uttering his lack of guts as he never did anything of that kind in life. When the old man corners him how he got courage to run away from home, he replies that it was guts. Nila challenges him, "without guts could you put them to shame? Could you leave home with just 3 rupees 75 paise? Could you tell stories about rats nibbling a dhoti?" (95).

When Bagala is thus challenged he tells how he should get guts recollecting a word from the past. After much coxing he utters, "Bastard... Bastard uncle. Bastard aunt. Bastard father-in-law. Bastard mother-in-law...And their daughter!...All are bastards!" (97). The old man encourages him to shout louder and louder to get courage. Nila dances with joy and hands over paper for him to write that magic word "bastard" which becomes like a sacred chant. Nila offers an envelope and the letter is enclosed.

The Stage Managers appear and give more information on Bagala's childhood and adolescence. When the exit the old man tells Bagala not to be afraid of meeting uncle and aunt as there was no reason to be bogged down. He promises to make the trip the following day. The old man applauds him for not stammering. He requests the old man to order him around. But he declines saying that such decisions on his part can't be done by orders. Bagala, pacing up and down, dishevels his hair. Looking afar, he starts singing, while Nila comes back and sits beside the old man. The old man is impressed by the song and asks if he has composed it. He had composed a couple of them and left them on the shelf behind the books at home which Nila brings out by magic.

The Stage Manager appears and takes the story to the following morning when Bagala's tongue is found more loosened as he became a bit more courageous. The old man tells him to keep Nila in his pocket lest people might bump into her or some car would run over her in the busy streets of Calcutta. Bagala strikes the lighter to let Nila disappear, and keeps it in his pocket. The old man advices him to call Nila whenever he needs, especially immediately after he enters his uncle's home. The old man blesses him uttering, "May goddess 'bastard' be ever awake on the tip of your tongue. Be careful about the bag on the *bus*...take care of the *lighter*. If the bag's lost, you'll get many such bags – if the *lighter's* with you" (101).

As Bagala and Old Man exit, the Stage Managers make their comments on the uncle's home where the angry father-in-law quarrels with them for having broken the marriage proposal. But they are confident that the boy would return soon, since he has no money with him. Being an honest and sincere boy they assure the man that he wouldn't steal or beg, instead would return. The man on his part threatens them to produce him within twenty four hours or return the advance of Rs. 5000/- taken from the dowry.

When Bagala reaches home along with Nila, he finds an enraged uncle and aunt. When the man questions if he would marry his daughter, Nila prompts him to agree to the proposal. Nila plays tricks on the man by tapping him on the shoulder. Irritated the man charges the uncle for disturbing him. She also taps him from the aunt's side and throws away the shawl from his shoulder. As the interrogation continues, Nila pushes the aunt who is caught by the uncle. The man expresses his disgust in their embracing each other. Nila next puts the man's shawl on Bagala. She keeps playing tricks pulling aunt's hair, tapping uncle's head and letting them into a monkey dance. The man gets annoyed with their crazy behaviour and surmises it to be a family trait. Facing Bagala, Nila shouts "Bastard," which he repeats to the shock of the man. Meanwhile, Nila pushes uncle who bumps into the man. As they fall to the ground, she pushes down aunt. When the man shouts for help, Bagala attempts to help but he is also pushed down. In the confusion the man makes his escape without his Rs.5000.

Taking out the letter from Bagala's pocket and handing it over to him, Nila prompts him to give his enraged uncle. His face toughens and he tears up the letter and speaks with courage: "Bastard? Son of a bitch? It must be. Otherwise why'd I suffer smacking and spanking in your hands for all these years? Yes. You're right. I'm a bastard. Son of a bitch" (105).

Uncle, aunt and Nila are transfixed and surprised at his expression. He tells them that he spoke directly what he had written in the letter and whatever he owed them he had repaid with hard work. Throwing the money bag at the uncle, he speaks in a rage, "There's ten thousand here. And listen – you bastard uncle!...If you aren't a son of a bitch yourself, return five thousand rupees to that gentleman" (106). As he exits in arrogance with Nila, she pinches uncle and aunt on their cheek and takes the man's shawl and puts on aunt's head. The couple gets shocked. When the uncle wonders who Nila is, his wife utters hysterically "Witch! Witch!...Our Bagai's bewitched!" (106).

The Stage Managers enter and push out uncle and aunt and exit crying and shouting. They comment on Bagala, the hero who has taken to the streets like a valiant victor. In his excitement he is completely unmindful of Nila. Putting her hand on his shoulders, Nila walks behind him, hiding herself. He drags her beside, walking arm-in-arm, endangering her in the busy street. Nila begs him to take her in his pocket. He strikes the lighter and she disappears. Observing him light the striker, a pedestrian reminds him that he had forgotten to put a cigarette in his mouth. When he replies that he doesn't smoke, the man thinks him crazily strike the lighter for light in the streets at noon.

Though the old man enters laughing, he is disappointed that Bagala had not given the letter. When the boy strikes the lighter, Nila enters and rushes to hold both his hands and twirls him around. As Nila lets him go, he tries to maintain balance and sits down. When the old man reminds him of the interview on Friday he shows his guts to attend it:

> BAGALA: I'll go all out!
> OLD MAN: With Nila's help…
> BAGALA: Don't need it. Go all out myself! Got to stand on my own feet!
> OLD MAN: Bravo! If all of your age could stand on their own feet, could say they'd go all out, then…
> BAGALA: The what?
> OLD MAN: Then the world wouldn't have been like this. We haven't learnt to stand up, never went to fight. We always think that everything will be changed by *magic*.
> BAGALA: *No magic*! *No* magic! Everything's to be done with one's own strength! With one's own hand! I'll tell everyone!
> NILA: Then don't you need me any longer, master?
> BAGALA (*startled*): You… with him…
> (*Puts forth the lighter to the OLD MAN*).
> OLD MAN: No. No. I won't take it anymore. I started depending too much on Nila. Now I too will stand on my own feet. Go all out!

Nila is confused as to what she would do henceforth. Bagala tells her to be his girlfriend. In the meantime, the old man decides to take a break for a month to go off to the Himalayas and other places of pilgrimage. But when Nila asks him how much money he requires, he declines her offer saying, "No money! No magic money! The money I earned is in the bank. I'll set off once you get a job. Both of you stay here. Look after my house. When she offers to do everything through her magical power, Bagala tells her that everything will be done with their own hands. When Nila reveals her helplessness in doing things by her own hands, he offers to teach everything which he had learnt in his uncle's home. When she fumbles he scolds and tells her, "Shut up! Stop stammering! Don't have to stand on your own feet?" (109). When the old man reminds him of the past when he had been to the railway tracks to commit suicide, Bagala reacts with sternness:

BAGALA: Bastard. Who needs to be on the railway tracks? *Sorry* I…OLD MAN: No *sorry*! Let Nila and 'bastard' be ever alive in your pocket and heart, respectively" (109).

The Stage Managers enter and inform how Bagala was rewarded with a job. The old man set off to the Himalayas. Bagala began to teach Nila cooking and other household chores. She finds it difficult even to peel onions, however, she shows her great patience. She exhorts him to sing the song he composed after getting the job. As he sings Nila joins too:

> BAGALA-NILA: Magic doesn't help a real attempt
> Do away with it at this moment
> Come with brooms, running
> Clean the filth by sweeping
> Sloth, coward, idler – all
> Brooms in your hands, have a ball (110).

Bagala's story brings to surface how human will and determination alone can make one stand on his own feet instead of living in a make-believe world of magic. The dramatist reaches out to his audience with a moral lesson in establishing ones own identity as a worthwhile human being, shedding built in inferiority complex under whatever oppressive circumstances. In the beginning of the play Bagala mentions about his desire to blow trumpet from childhood, referring to his desire to bloom and mature as a normal child. But the opportunity was denied him due to accidental death of his parents, leading to a warped life at his uncle's home. His in feriority complex continues to be established at school and college when he is looked down upon by jeering peers and teachers. His decision to escape from life by suicide is thwarted by the magical assistance of the old man. In course of time, he is transformed by the magical life he lives with Nila, who instills courage in him through the promptings of his mentor. Once he matures in self confidence, the old man challenges him to stand on his own feet, shedding a magical solution to solve his angst. He proves that it is only acquired guts and courage that can lead one to self determination. In the final analysis, Bagala sheds the power of magic to live a normal life, challenging his own diffidence and fear of those who suppressed him. Success dawns when he relies on his own will and determination.

Sircar has been probing into the meaninglessness of life which the existentialists refer to as *Angst* or *anguish* a Germanic word for fear or anxiety. Heidegger's *Sein und Zeit* could be rendered as *Anxiety, uneasiness* or *malaise* suggesting our daily anxieties. For Kierkegaard *Angst* meant *dread* while for Sartre *anguish* (Macquarrie 164-5). Kierkegaard's *Angst* (*dread*) describes an innate spiritual state of insecurity and despair. According to him, "anxiety is a qualification of dreaming spirit, and as such it has its place in psychology.... In anxiety it (innocence) is related to the forbidden and to the punishment. Innocence is not guilty, yet there is anxiety as though it were lost..." (Kierkegaard 41- 5). It is angst that frustrates the protagonist, leading him to run away from home and attempt suicide.

The playwright seems to borrow from the absurdists for whom reality being meaningless, life is reduced to a mere circular progress from nothing to nothing. The true field of battle is inside us, in the Unconscious. Hence Sircar attacks us below the threshold of consciousness using mainly visual devices and language in a state of fragmentation. His concern is with the doomed individual, the man in despair and distress, alone and bitter in the wide world (Sebastian 15). The dramatist very deftly confronts his audience with harsh facts of isolated life in an alien world.

The playwright has been very successful bringing to focus various aspects of unconventional free theatre. In his creativity, he has been inspired by the art of Bernard Shaw, Moliere and O'Neill. His fusion of farce, nonsense, existential and absurd elements, render his plays differ from the conventional naturalistic drama, as he claimed, "My plays are never naturalistic. Invariably too, they deal with a human situation or problem. I realized long ago that I wasn't cut out to be a novelist. Writers can analyze individual human beings from a point of detachment. I haven't looked at life that way" ("Off Stage."http://www.indiaprofile.com).

Third Theatre has been successful since it establishes the intimacy of sharing an experience with the audience with free play of imagination, manifested through symbolic costumes. It also provides freedom to perform within the arena format with the intense use of body language which has immense possibilities as the body relates to one's consciousness, emotions and knowledge ("Off Stage."http://www.indiaprofile.com).

Works Cited:

"Bada Sircar "http://www.indianetzone.com/ 33 bada l_sircar _indian _theatre_personality.htm

Kierkegaard, Soren. *Anxiety as the Presupposition of Hereditary Sin.* Trans. Reidar Thomte. New Jersey: Princeton University Press, 1980.

Lal, Ananda. Ed. *Theatres of India.* New Delhi: Oxford University Press, 2009.

Macquarrie, John. *Existentialism.* New York: Penguin Books, 1972.

"Off Stage."http://www.indiaprofile.com/people/badalsircar.htm.

Sebastian, A.J. & N.D.R. Chandra. *Literary Terms in Drama Theatre and Cinema.* Delhi: Authorspress, 2002.

Sircar, Badal. *Two Plays.* New Delhi: Oxford University Press, 2009 (Abbreviated: *TP*).

12

Class Antagonism in Manoj Mitra's *Honey from a Broken Hive*

Manoj Mitra (1938 -), Bengali actor, director and dramatist emerged as a dramatist of great calibre with popular plays such as *Chak Bhanga Modhu, Sajano Bagan, Rajdarshan, Kinu Kaharer Thetar, Alakanandar Putrakanya, Darpane Sharatshashi* and *Galpo Hekimshaheb*. His plays have been remarkable in depicting human alienation and the cruelty of powerful classes (Lal 270-1). Mitra has been very innovative in combining humour and pathos while depicting history, mythology, fantasy, and reality in his plays.

Indian People's Theatre Association (IPTA) formed in 1943, stressing people's struggle for freedom, cultural progress and economic justice, had established its unit in Bengal propounding leftist views and ideals (Lal 162-3). In Bengal IPTA came to be *Gana Natya* which gave freshness to theatre, drawing the attention of the audience with its political message. Theatre became a movement against established order of society involving problems of common man. Theatre established close affinity with contemporary political, social, economic and cultural changes in Bengal. *Gana Natya* adhered to Marxist ideology and exposition of the class struggle leading to resistance and violence. It is in this context that Mitra's plays ought to be examined since his style emerges from a distinctive philosophy of being. Many of his plays belong to people's theatre and not political theatre. From political theatre, he turned towards a theatre of conscience in *Chhayar Prashad, Galpo Hekimshaheb* and *Chak Bhanga Modhu*, moving towards alternate frames of resistance and freedom from oppression *Chak Bhanga Modhu*(1969) depicts the period of Naxal Movement in Bengal, examines the problem of representation (*TTOC* 1-4).

In the late 1960s and early 1970s, the Naxalite movement was immensely popular. On 2March 1967, a tribal youth named Bimal Kissan from a remote Naxalbari village in West Bengal obtained a judicial order with the right to plough his land. The local landlord attacked him with the help of his goons. The tribals of the area retaliated and started forcefully recapturing their lands. Thus began the Naxal movement into which even brilliant students, dropping out of college, joined in the struggle for the rights of the tribals and landless labourers ("Birth of Naxalism."http: www.competitionmaster.com).

Mitra's response to politically motivated violence and killing of landlords is summed up in his plays. He recounts how he created his characters:

> Matla and Badami of *Honey from a Broken Hive* I have seen from very close. I have seen the rags in which they cover themselves... Poverty was their constant friend. They never thought of freedom. Poverty seemed to be a deadly illness that enveloped them like a deep coma. Around the 1970s I read somewhere in the newspapers, 'Man goes to *ojha's* house to take out poison and dies of snakebite.' It was then that I wrote *Honey from a Broken Hive*. In *Honey from a Broken Hive* there was a snake in Matla Ojha's house as well. But Aghor Ghosh does not die of snakebite. He gives his life to Badami's machete. In the play, the news changed only that much. The news was a catalyst for writing the play. Had it not been for that piece of news, perhaps I would never have written the play (*TTOC* 24).

The story surrounds Matla Ojha who is a snake tamer who is able to treat people suffering from snakebites. His power of sorcery helps him to heal and destroy people. The victim brought to him for treatment is his bitter class opponent, Aghor Ghosh, who has taken over his land and property. However, he treats the man for ethical reasons than political vendetta. Mitra also depicts violence in the midst of extreme poverty. The play presents moral choice in the midst of conflict and violence, bringing to focus consciousness that goes beyond the closures of binaries of the regulating norms of the political theatre (4-6).

The play is replete with symbolic language depicting conflict and violence in the community of *ojhas* of Sunderbans who work with snakes and snake venom. The snake and its poison runs through as a powerful symbol throughout. Poison spreads all over the text of the play. Having mastery over poison controls life and death. Matla Ojha wields such a power over the landlord Aghor, through his magic chants (25).

The play opens at the tumbledown hut of Matla Ojha where his daughter Badami sleeps in the courtyard to the chirping of wild birds. Matla returns home after a weary day's labour by the slopes of the ridge. The half- naked, rugged old man has on his head a clay pot.

The conversation between Badami and Matla gives cue to their impoverished life. Badami is upset Matla was out the whole day leaving her all alone. She wants to know if he brought any grain. He tells her not to strain herself, to protect the babe in her womb. She is curious to know what he has brought in the pot. He makes her guess what it could be - Cane gur? Juice of tal? Honey? He tells her he found two huge hives in the forests of Godaho on a high branch, hidden among leaves.

As he speaks of the way bees chased him, old Jata enters, hoping to satisfy his hunger with the honey. When Badami hurriedly opens the lid, she screams and jumps back in fright, finding a baby Cobra instead. Matla consoles her that she wouldn't die, hailing from the family of *ojhas* who are snake handlers. He came across the snake when he went in search of food. When he was about to spit, he found the snake coiled around his feet as though it came out of his chest. Badami trembling with fear, accuses him for having brought a snake, telling it to be honey from a broken hive. She hurls herself at Matla and tears his hair with her hands, indicating perhaps her incestuous relationship, in the absence of her husband who left her. Poverty had made him barely able to walk, making him almost crawl on his chest like a snake. Old Jata recounts how Badami's grandma starved for seventeen days and then jumped into the river to end her life with a godly smile of a faithful wife. On the contrary, Badami utters only poisonous words. Jata suggests to terminate her pregnancy with the assistance of the village woman. It was a shocking news for both Matla and Badami, who show their respect for human life:

> MATLA: Uncle! You ask me to kill a human being?
> JATA: Yes, yes, I do...
> MATLA: (*Pounces on Jata*). You damned creature, you still

move about because I give you a share of my earnings! And you dare- (122).

An enraged Matla drives out old Jata threatening to break his legs for prompting to clean her womb. He consoles Badami that he would never kill the child before birth, and would collect money from moneylenders even by mortgaging the land.

Soon an excited Jata comes to inform that moneylender Aghor Ghosh is on his way to Matla's home. Presuming it to be a visit to grab all he could holding the red book in his hand. Since Matla owes him a lot of money, he plans to hide in the garden. When Jata reveals that Aghor is dying of snakebite, he is glad he would die and would never return to collect hundred rupees he owes him. He starts dancing with joy at the good news. A Muslim farmer, details how Aghor was bitten by a very poisonous snake while he was resting after the midday meal. He is surprised to see them making merry instead of going with him to the dying man. Good moral sense prevails over Badami who pleads with her father to heal the man.

> BADAMI: Won't you take the poison off him?... Don't you know, the *ojha* himself must rush to the ailing as soon as he hears of poisoning Come on…
> MATLA: Uncle, what's this girl to say? The person who's robbed me of everything… I'll go, take the poison off him!
> BADAMI: What are you saying? The man's dying!
> MATLA: God's taking him, eh! And I'll snatch him from His mouth? Won't that be wrong. Uncle?
> JATA: 'Course it'll be. Like scratching yourself to make a rash.
> BADAMI: Are you human or… If Pa don't come, you do old man… Do you hear me? *Ojhas*, all of you… (127).

The sequence is indicative of her moral responsibility to a dying man, which she maintains through out the play.

The party of Aghor comes along with his son Shankar, a young business man. Though Matla is called out several times, he doesn't respond. Jata gives different excuses saying that the man has gone to market to buy fish and vegetables, to make rice pudding for his daughter. Shankar requests the old Jata to go and heal his father. He declines the offer saying he had forgotten the magic chants. In the meantime, Badami enters with a clay dish in her hands containing some rice. She assures Shankar that he needn't fear since her father would treat him. She informs that Matla is at home, to the utter surprise of all. Shankar asks her not to fret about the petty troubles of the past. He promises to give them due reward or money for the services.

Badami reminds her father about the big expenses he has to incur as her time to give birth is drawing near. She tells him to save the master to get all the money he needs. She expresses her fears and terrible pain in her body. Matla finally relents to her demands and decides to save the man.

In Act II, Jata, Badami and Matla gather in a corner of the ridge where the palanquin bearers bring Aghor. Jata pours a thin stream of water on Matla's hands and approach the palanquin. Jata asks for mustard oil and bananas for the ritual to begin. Matla asks for a fishing rod as well, which comes as a surprise to everyone. Jata gets annoyed and tells him to say how far the poison has moved. As the commotion goes on, Shankar enters dismissing the palanquin bearers, arguing with Matla. Badami comes in with a basket full of creepers and hading over to her father assures that a man bitten by snakes can live for seven days. Shankar is confident that the *ojha* would heal his father in due time. Unable to bear Badami's powerful gaze, Matla fretfully yells at her to leave as poison would never leave the body when a woman is around. As she obliges and returns to the hut, Matla tells Jata that they could run away with the money they had already extorted for buying various articles for the ritual. Matla intents to tell them to call someone else to remove the poison, knowing full well none could do it. Matla doesn't want the man to survive, lest he continues harassing them by taking over their land. "I feel I've slipped into a larger bugger of a trap myself! Neither can we chant nor can we let others go near him fearing he comes round! The man's dying but still he won't spare us!" (154).

Matla suggests to Shankar to take his father away from there if he wishes to save his life. Hearing this, Badami begs her father not to kill the man.

> BADAMI: So why kill now?
> MATLA: I kill?
> BADAMI: Don't you? His life's in your hands and you don't give it to him.

MATLA: No!
BADAMI: You have no powers!
MATLA: What!
BADAMI: Yes, yes, it was your pa that brought the medals… but you learnt nothing from him!...O, Pa, stop it! How can he, on whose yard a man dies, claim to be an *ojha*?
MATLA: Dies! Then behold if I can save him or not!

Being, challenged to be a deserving *ojha*, Matla rushes to the dying man and runs roots over him. Immediately Badami observes poison going down and darkness and poison leaving him. She is found to be in excruciating pain and experiences something jumping in her body. Matla tells her to sit quiet and lie on his thighs to stop the bugger in her from jumping around. Badami on her part requests her father to keep chanting as the master twitches his mouth with life coming back to him.

When Jata makes his entry, he feels as though he has seen a ghost. He rushes to Matla and strikes his face with roots and creepers. Badami observes poison rise and fall like a dangerous game of dance. Jata pulls out Aghor's hand and tries to tear off the shining gold medal. Badami chases him with a bamboo to hit on the head calling him a corpse eating vulture. Matla, on his part has become like an immovable stone. However, he begins to move and suddenly runs to get a pot of toddy and drinks till he becomes drunk with laughter and shouts, "This bloody poison's like a wild cow that enters the garden and destroys everything!" ((159). As he continues in his drunken state, Shankar questions Badami why they do nothing to heal. She expresses their inability to do anything and tells him to take the master elsewhere. When Shankar questions her further why they are unwilling to heal, she lets out the truth that they have fear of saving the master. Shankar, being aware of the truth of the matter, agrees with her:

SHANKAR: That's right! How can they? Bloodsucking vampire of a moneylender…

BADAMI: Master! Master!, I don't know what made you say that… but none of it's untrue! That one man alone has destroyed this entire village… You're so good…even your own pa you…

> SHANRKAR: Why my pa? I don't fear even his pa when it comes to speaking the truth. We're shop keepers…We deal with folks like you. Don't we understand your pains? Just the other day Harish from Balarampur had come… (163).

The moment her husband Harish's name is uttered, she gets excited to know his whereabouts. Shankar gives details of how he thinks about her and the child to be born. He borrowed some money from Shankar and bought a pair of silver bangles for the baby. He is growing crops and would take her and the baby after harvesting. Badami is moved with emotion hearing the good news. Shankar asks her to attempt trying the chants and the ritual, to bring Aghor to life and then reveal the truth of all the injustice he has committed.

> SHANKAR: …Once he's dead, it'll be over. What's to Aghor Ghosh? He'll be set free by death and never know the harm he's done the lot of you. So much harm he's brought on you…won't you tell him? Save him… make him stand up… then tell him, 'Master, look, I could have let you die… but I gave you back your life!' Now, won't that be revenge?... He'll bow before you…he'll die knowing it was the snakebite that killed him… Poverty made Harish leave you. I'll make Aghor Ghosh take care of your poverty…You save Aghor Ghosh. I'll see to it that Harish, you and the baby are able to live. And live well! (164-5).

With hope in her eyes, she picks up the roots to make the chants. Matla makes his entry and warns that if she touches Aghor the poison will go to her womb and make the child become like the poisoned man. She tells him not to scold her for doing a good work, but pleads with him to save him: "Pa, aren't you an *ojha*! Such is the magic of your hands. If you cast your spell twice, the poison goes down in a jiffy… Sometimes, I want to drink poison and give myself to your chants and spells… in the hands of a *gunin* like you" (166). Her affirmation of his power as a medicine man possessing magical powers, sets Matla to make arrangements for reciting the chants. He thrusts his hands inside and runs them swiftly over Aghor's body, chasing the venom out with his slaps. By and by Aghor's arms, legs and head begins to move. Aghor begins to crawl like an animal. Matla takes the creeper and shakes at Aghor's feet. He cries out in joy and grief and throws himself before the palanquin. He has marks all over his body as he writhes in intense heat. Matla refuses to give any water. He directs Badam to get fire on him. Aghor is laid on a bamboo platform under which fire is kept. Dakkhayani, his whore, assists Aghor to open his mouth to swallow heat. Dakkhayani reminds him how she had warned him, "A thousand times've told you, be careful. Is there a dearth of enemies? How you make a mess of anything I don't attend to… Eat, live and live in peace… How many times I've told you, don't sleep in the courtyard. Five hundred-so-many sacks piled there. Who knows what creatures lurk… no, he must sleep there and hold guard. Why? Don't we guard them? No, he won't listen. He'll do exactly what we tell him not to" (169). She feels so broken that he has reached such a stage.

Matla comes forward asking Aghor how he feels after he had been pulled out from the jaws of a tiger. He tells him that he has nothing to fear of Ma Manasha (one eyed goddess of snakes) as long as he wears the string on his neck. He also tells him that while reciting the chants he had done away with his own poison.

OLD DULI-BEARER: Your poison!

MATLA: Yes, yes. Mine! Listen to me. Hatred for you had poisoned my heart…How often I've thought 'Let me lay hands on him just once.' You've taken our land, mortgaged our homestead, made us toil for free… Master, you even killed my old pig and sold its meat when I couldn't pay…And yet your debts remained unpaid. Stamping over the heart of this village, you've sucked its blood. Caught us tight in the net of fresh debts day after day… Now that you've gotten your own life back, d' you know that we too have a life!... mine own poison went down with yours! A new life for you… a new life for me too… (170).

When Aghor gets back to his senses, he begins to question why he had not been attended to when writhing in pain for so long. He is all the more annoyed as to why he had been carried there instead of the *ojha* treating him in his own home. When he sees Matla, Aghor demands his interest.

> AGHOR: Pay my interest!
> MATLA: Interest!
> AGHOR: Give back my *taka*! Tried to kill me, cheat me…
> MATLA: Master!
> DAKKA & SHANKAR: Right!

AGHOR: Kill me! Devil! Give me my *taka*!
MATLA: What do you want, Master? Interest?
SHANKAR: (*takes his shoe in his hand and starts roaring*) Pleading at the feet of these swines was all that was left for me to do…
AGHOR: (*in drunken swoon*) Not give me? No? I'll take your all… You thought I was dead! All had ended! (171-2).

When Badami enters, gritting his teeth, Aghor approaches her with sexual demands. Dakkhayani warns him the woman is pregnant. As he goes to the palanquin, he tells Dakkhayani to get the woman to his house to live with him. She tells Badami to oblige the master who lives lonely without a wife. She would always have food, clothing and shoal fish, in return. Besides, people would forget whether she is Brahmin or lowborn within a couple of days. Matla begs not to take his daughter away and pleads his helplessness in front of all. Badami decides to go with the master saying that she is moving to her in-law's. When Matla reacts sternly she retorts that she won't be beaten and abused by him anymore.

Aghor taunts and derides Matla for having plotted to kill him. When he reaches the ridge, he notices Dakkhayani squatting there. He chases her with a stick as she had tries to grab his wealth by keeping his keys. When she flees in despair, Badami steps out with a pot of honey. When Matla remonstrates in terror, he is grabbed by the palanquin bearers who stuff cloth into his mouth to silence him. Badami tells Aghor since he can't drink water, she has the pot of honey from two large hives on the gab tree in the forests of Godaho. When he longs to drink the honey from her hands she says, "If Pa could give you life, why can't I give you honey? Drink some and cool yourself" (176). When Matla tries to snatch the pot away, Aghor pounces on it and pulls it on to his lap. When he opens the lid of the pot to look inside, Badami clutches her father's hand and jumps in joy, presuming the snake to rise to fang Aghor to death. Matla reveals that he had killed the snake earlier. Snatching the pot in great anguish, Badami smashes it on the floor. Laughing and crying like a mad woman, she drags the snake as if she were disembowelling herself. After lashing the snake on the ground a few times, she runs to pick up the tortoise-killing machete and rushes to Aghor. Unable to make his escape, being surrounded by the villagers, Badami swings at him and tears his chest with her own hands. Drums of *gajon* (festival of Shiva) could be heard as Matla holds her to his chest, ending the drama.

It is in her helplessness that Badami strikes the man dead, when he demands her, a pregnant woman to be his whore, in compensation for money due to him. Matla on his part proves his moral sense to revive the wicked Aghor, in spite of impoverishing him and the villagers.

Comparisons can be made between the unconscious snakebite the wicked Aghor suffers, rendering him a swollen monster and Badami's pregnant body, ripe with child (26). As the poison is being removed from the dying man, Badami groans in agony with the child in her moving ferociously. The sequence shows the contrast of the two characters. Aghor continues to be evil through and through, while Badami maintains her moral obligation to save his life.

The dilemma in the play is whether to save the snake-bitten Aghor or let him die who is a social menace. The play powerfully portrays class antagonism (26). Snake and pot of honey are symbolic of eroticism leading to death. Poison in Bengali language signifies seduction (27). When the poison is being removed by Matla, Badami feels proud of her father and wants to drink poison and hand herself into his chants and spells.

The play belongs to Theatre of conscience which draws attention to judge between 'Where lies violence?' and 'What is justice?' unlike in the political theatre where it is violence that decides justice as per ideologies. However, Mitra's theatre of conscience doesn't get trapped in ideological positions (8). At the end after killing the wicked Aghor, Badami establishes the value of life (27).

The play could also be viewed from the standpoint of Ethical Criticism which analyses the potential moral effects of stories on a reader and to assess how such effects occur. Most fiction represent real life, and real life inevitably requires moral judgements and standards. Current Postmodern theory cannot avoid the "ethical" merely renaming it "political" or "rhetorical." Ethical criticism helps readers see, understand and appreciate the powerful ways in which fictions invite them into specific ways of feeling, thinking, and judging, a process that ultimately exerts a powerful influence on readers' hearts and minds (Gregory 37). Though Mitra presents through the play social antagonism in the backdrop of the misery of landless poor leading to Naxal movement, he, draws attention to moral and the immoral in the lives of people. Even the impoverished village people depicted in the play such as Badami and Matla, show their exceptional moral calibre. However, "good life requires a favourable social context... Socially desirable human behaviour is not genetically programmed or instinctive. Socially desirable behaviour must be socially encouraged. Society must set and enforce moral rules, just as it must set and enforce rules" (Olson 143). Though the play brings class antagonism to the fore, it establishes social and moral obligations typical of the theatre of conscience.

Works Cited

"Birth of Naxalism." http://www.competitionmaster.com/ArticleDetail.aspx?ID=2473333f-24e3-48b7-b307-7ee00adda69c

Gregory, Marshall. "Ethical Criticism: What It Is and Why It Matters." *Ethics, Literature, Theory*. Ed. Stephen K. George. Maryland: Rowman & Littlefield Publishers, 2005.

Lal, Ananda. *The Oxford Companion to Indian Theatre*. New Delhi: Oxford University Press, 2004.

Mitra, Manoj. "Honey from a Broken Hive." *The Theatre of Conscience*. Calcutta: Seagull Books, 2007, 115-178. (Abbreviated *TTOC*).

Olson, Robert G. *Ethics: A Short Introduction*. New York: Routledge, 1978.

13

Enigma Surrounding a Woman's Identity in Mahesh Elkunchwar's *Garbo*

Marathi dramatist Mahesh Elkunchwar has been successful in portraying human predicament in the face of death, loneliness and illusions of all kinds, leading to apparent purposelessness of choice as the ultimate goal of life remaining unknown (Lal 120). In writing his play *Garbo*, he has probed into the meaningless lives young people live in our contemporary society, devoid of social and ethical values. According to him the young generation depicted in the play revolted against imposed traditions, seeking freedom. But they were disillusioned as Elkunchwar opined: "Suddenly the non-conformists among us had decided to shake off all this artificial baggage imposed on us by tradition. At the same time we had realized that we didn't know what to do with the freedom...Since we were not equipped to use this freedom creatively and constructively, we began to destroy ourselves in the process" (Bandyopadhyay xii). He is concerned with sexuality as the central issue as he probes into the inner battles of his characters (xii). Shrimant, Intuc and Pansy merely use Garbo for their sexual satisfaction with no genuine affection for her. The three men indulge in their sexual fantasies with Garbo as they come together on a Sunday morning. The three men have different attitude towards her. For Shrimant she is merely a sex machine, giving him sexual satisfaction. Intuc observes her as a living work of art while Pansy sees her like an older sister. The scenes portray comic acting by the characters. The comic situation becomes grim when she announces her pregnancy. They all shrug off their responsibility and Garbo lets the babe in her womb get aborted accidentally.

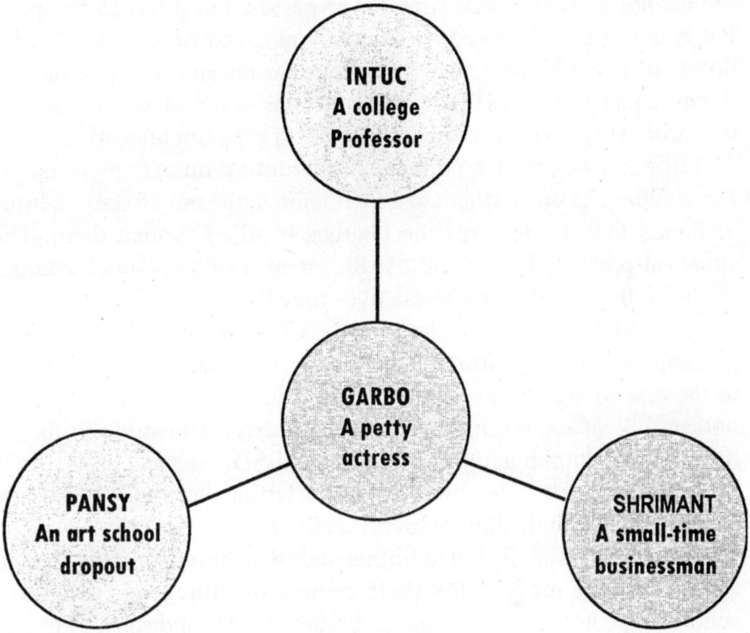

Garbo may be examined in the absurd tradition. The absurdists have no story or plot, no recognizable characters, no proper theme with a beginning and end. They reflect dreams and nightmares with incoherent babbling (Esslin 21-22).

The play opens as Pansy and Intuc are relaxing in a room. Pansy is fiddling with a radio to listen to his favourite Hindi songs. He recollects how as a boy he used to listen to radio songs outside a pan shop. Intuc on his part recounts how he used to listen to classical music and go to concerts where he used to clap hands the longest. Now that he is a Professor, he has to pretend to understand classical music. He speaks of the modern trend by which people pretend to be interested in music. "Those days are gone, kiddo, when you could enjoy music as a private pleasure. Nowadays these musical conferences are an immense fraud perpetrated by the community upon the community... You've got everything there except good music" (*CPME* 5-6). Their assessment of concerts becomes sexy as Pansy suggests that Intuc arranges for a private concert to enjoy the company of sexy women.

The two men find it boring awaiting the arrival of Shrimant. Intuc philosophises saying that time never passes, but it has to be spent. Pansy expresses his boredom being a young boy of seventeen. Intuc boasts of his achievement writing four stories and four poems, and winning instant fame. He also dedicated his new collection of poems to Garbo. He reflects on fame as "a sort of pleasant allegation" (8).

Shrimant enters as a policeman, disrupting Intuc's discourse on fame. When he orders them to go with him to the police station, Intuc demands that he declares the charges levelled against them. The situation presented is absurd as Shrimant levels his mock charges exposing the world of valueless lives they live:

SHRIMANT: ... You are guilty of using impossibly clean language shorn of all obscenities, thus causing acute embarrassment to those who are in the habit of using abusive language... You are both guilty of expressing contempt and disgust towards drinking, meat-eating, smoking, opium, hemp, and LSD...Instead of having a bit of fun with good-looking chicks and letting them go, you soppily indulge in pure and sublime love... (10).

In the mock trial Shrimant further adds that Intuc and Pansy would be given gold medals for their crimes of "integrity, extensive scholarship, ardent selflessness, boundless philanthropy, humble service, burning patriotism and an unblemished character" (11). The mock trial ends and Shrimant demands drinks. When he is unable to get it, he quarrels with Pansy and Intuc. The duo decides to leave when Shrimant tells them to get out of his house. As they are about to leave Shrimant gives Pansy a parcel containing cufflinks. He apologises for having misbehaved with them and begs them to stay on with him. When Intuc questions him on his sudden outbursts, Shrimant refers to it as sentimentality as has been pointed out by Garbo. But Pansy points out how rational Garbo is by not losing her emotional balance.

The conversation shifts to Garbo whom Shrimant describes as a woman who is always available and very great in bed. When Pansy confirms her as a great woman, Shrimant calls him a humorist. He goes on to describe her as a sex-machine. Pansy shows his annoyance at such derogatory remarks. Intuc points out how Shrimant contradicts himself. "Now, if she is a machine, she is devoid of emotions. And if she is devoid of emotions, she can't be great in bed"

(16). Pansy objects to Shrimant calling Garbo a common whore. Intuc philosophises and says, "...Names don't change things. Garbo will remain Garbo, while we will continue to search for the kind of Garbo we want. If we find her, well and good. If we don't we will suffer a bit. Or not even that, after a while" (17). Shrimant refuses to suffer and would instead look for someone else in her place. Intuc points out to "let Garbo be what she is. The important thing is to know what we are...But I know what I want from her...Garbo is a challenge. She grows older but never stale" (18). He wonders what would be the secret of her great quality. He surmises her to be a great artist persevering in her infinite freshness. Her freshness may be compared to the infinite variety of Shakespeare's Cleopatra.

The conversation leads to their further comments on the enigma surrounding women. Shrimant opines that women can never go stale. But Intuc is of the opposite viewpoint and makes his derogatory remarks: "Once you've understood a woman, you don't want to look at her again. Once you've explored her the thrill is gone. A woman should be able to satisfy you fully, and yet withhold a part of herself from you" (18). Shrimant wants the Professor to sum up his thoughts on Garbo into 'Garbo-Slut and Enigma' (18). Intuc puts things in perspective when he says that part of Garbo remains untouched even after satisfying all three of them. She proves to be a great artist in her dealing with people queuing outside her house including film producers, directors and cameramen. According to Shrimant, she is a whore who receives everyone into her enigmatic embrace.

When news arrives that Garbo is about to come, the three men are excited to meet her. The conversation gives leads into the kind of relationship between the four.

> PANSY: Garbo is here.
>
> ...
>
> SHRIMANT: Now three cheers for Garbo the sex-machine. Come on. Darling Garbo.
>
> ...
>
> PANSY: We've been waiting for you for hours.
> GARBO: But I hadn't said I'd come.
> PANSY: Even then we were waiting (20-1).

She decides to take Pansy along with her, considering him a child who had run away from his home and attempted suicide. Shrimant comments on it as her wanting to have a toy with her. Intuc makes his absurd comment on suicide: "Thus Pansy allowed a golden opportunity to slip through his fingers. Pansy this is the time. You're at the right age for a beautiful deed, like suicide. Later on a man becomes thick-skinned, and continues to cling to life shamelessly like a leach" (22).

Garbo is unhappy with Intuc telling the boy such dreadful things and tells Pansy not to pay any heed to such promptings. The conversation leads to their accusing each other and speaking of Garbo as a chaste woman.

> SHRIMANT: Honey, since when have you started objecting to our laying on you?
> GARBO: You have a dirty mind.
> INTUC: And a dirty body as well.
> PANSY: You're disgusted, aren't you?
> INTUC: Disgusted is the word since Garbo is basically a pure, chaste creature and all that.
> GARBO: of course I am.
> INTUC: A chaste woman of chaste family living in a chaste, tradition-bound society, once gave birth to another chaste woman… (24).

The three men speak of the emptiness they experience in their lives, while Garbo claims having no emptiness in her as she would be a mother soon. The three men put their ears to her stomach and make derogatory remarks. Intuc goes to the extent of saying that she would become a mother of three babes of good fortune like Dattaguru incarnate. Garbo shed tears showing her sensitivity to their ugly remarks. She bursts out: "Go away. Don't slobber over me like a dog. And don't call me Garbo again either…Are you trying to merely flaunt my failure before me? I'm aware of my failure, perhaps better than you. And I'm trying to come to terms with it. I don't claw at people, draw blood, and then dance with demonic joy the way you do" (27).

When Garbo makes towards the door to go away, Pansy pleads with her not to leave, acknowledging their mistake. She surrenders in humility as a whore in their presence, telling them to continue with their game. Shrimant taunts her being mawkish and sentimental. Intuc calls it her escape mechanism and sentimentality. She agrees to be with them to play their game provided they desisted from annoying her further. She asks the three men to play with her – the game of the slut and the three gentlemen. They begin to play a game imitating each other to feel alive.

Intuc imitates a neighbour Tatya who calls himself a holy man who has lived with his paralysed and blind wife for fifty years and never strayed from the path of morality. He caresses Garbo affectionately calling her like his own daughter. He tells her to keep off from the company of the libertines. The game further leads to the others pulling out Intuc's dhoti, exposing his nakedness.

Suddenly, Garbo becomes serious and tells them that they are all wallowing filth. Shrimant points out how she becomes emotional once again. Intuc has his justification as he says everything is filthy all around: "Can you show me a single place that is clean?... There's none left. If we are wallowing in filth, there's no escape for us. We must continue to live in this same filth. And we will say this filth is beautiful. In order to render this filth endurable, we will have to make up new theories about beauty… A sort of aesthetics of filth and depravity" (34). Garbo is annoyed at such comments and sulks when Intuc further slights her motherhood. He wonders why she should be telling them about her pregnancy when she is used to it being a whore. He suspects her trying to put the responsibility on them. He is in no mood to accept paternity. Garbo only spites them for their attitude towards her after having exploited her sexually all the time. The moment she is pregnant, they all consider her a cheap slut. She reminds them: "We'll allow ourselves to forget those days when you followed me around like dogs and couldn't do without me. .. I haven't come here to throw myself on your mercy. I don't want any help from you… But today I've seen you in your true colour" (36). Though she could implicate all of them in her pregnancy, she only wanted them to show her sympathy as a true friend. She demanded ten thousand rupees to abort the foetus. When Shrimant offers her the money she refuses saying he is not involved in it. When Intuc offers a cheque, she slaps it on his face in disgust. As she is about to leave, Intuc asks her pardon for behaving like a cad. She shrugs her shoulders and utters that it is her responsibility to find a way out. He begs her to let him have the child. He would look after it as penance for exploiting her sexuality.

INTUC: Yes. And we will humble ourselves before him. He will be our creation. And we will bow our heads before our own creation. A single smile from him will move us (*pleading*). Garbo let us do this. We are doomed people, we have neither seen, nor experienced, nor created anything beyond filth. Let us grab this opportunity. It's our only hope, our only chance. We will create something beautiful out of this filth. The world will know that there is a life somewhere which is beautiful, pure, fearless innocent... And Garbo, we cannot achieve this without you (40).

Garbo agrees to his proposal, but questions him if they would have the guts to pursue their decision. She would have to cancel all the contracts for an year taking maternity leave to nurture her babe – the beautiful thing in her life. Intuc reassures her that she won't have to work as he would see to all her needs. Her only job would be to love and nurse the child.

On her part, she expresses her longing to love someone and to lose herself in love. She asserts her need to be affirmed:

GARBO: There's a heap of ashes within me. Will I find one live ember in it? I have no
more strength left. Will I be able to live intensely again? (41)

Intuc reassures her that her life would bloom again. He invites her to stand in the middle and they all bow before her in great respect uttering in unison:

SHRIMANT, INTUC, PANSY: You are life.
The spring of fearless-beauty,
the source of all hope,
the fulfilment of all promises
are you. You are the beginning of belief.
You are the everlasting.
All future Suns are in your womb.
Give us your light.
...
He will be creation out of destruction.
Mother!
Mother!
Mother! (42).

In Act II, a month later, when preparations are made for the arrival of a baby, Garbo breaks the tragic news that her babe was aborted in the course of shooting a movie, while riding on a camel. Hearing the news, Intuc realises how undeserving the men are to see a child's birth. He acknowledges his sin:

INTUC: Let's return to filth. The world we desired was not for us, could never have been. We are idiots, out to turn dreams into reality. Let us go back to our old world now. The world of filth. As a punishment. As a sort of consolation too (49).

The three men beg her not to leave them in the lurch in that situation of abandonment. When she walks out of their lives, in despair Shrimant plunges a knife into her. As the play ends Intuc speaks out in despair : "Garbo's gone. Murdered. Or did she die first and was murdered later?" (66). He sums up the aimless life of mediocrity they live, exploiting women. Intuc's remarks pinpoints how Garbo died many a death before her murder, as a victim of man's lust. She is an enigmatic 'everywoman' losing her feminine identity in a male dominated society.

Garbo as a play portrays a "generation which breaks out into defiance of living out their own lives with non-conformism for a credo; throwing up in the process a small minority culture, containing within itself its own seeds of destruction. The drama in Garbo grows out of a claustrophobic real-life situation pushed to the limits of endurance..." ("Garbo."http://www.metawards.com). The drama is surrealistic and bizarre portrayal of contemporary society in which a class of young people live unethical lives in an enigmatic world of their making.

Works Cited:

Bandyopadhyay, Samik. "Introduction." *Collected Plays of Mahesh Elkunchwar*. New Delhi: Oxford University Press, 2009.

Elkunchwar, Mahesh. *Collected Plays of Mahesh Elkunchwar*. New Delhi: Oxford University Press, 2009. Abbreviated: *CPME.*

Esslin, Martin. *The Theatre of the Absurd*. London: Penguin. 1968.

"Garbo". http://www.metawards.com/plays/2010/garbo/.

Lal, Ananda. Ed. *The Oxford Companion to Indian Theatre*. New Delhi: Oxford University Press, 2004.

Index

***